MEN:

An International Anthology of African and Latin American Writers,
Volume 3

Edited by Tendai Rinos Mwanaka
Ingrid Bringas

Mwanaka Media and Publishing Pvt Ltd,
Chitungwiza Zimbabwe
*
Creativity, Wisdom and Beauty

Publisher: MMAP
Mwanaka Media and Publishing Pvt Ltd (Mmap)
24 Svosve Road, Zengeza 1
Chitungwiza Zimbabwe
mwanaka@yahoo.com
www.africanbookscollective.com/publishers/mwanaka-media-and-publishing
https://facebook.com/MwanakaMediaAndPublishing/

Distributed in and outside N. America by African Books Collective
orders@africanbookscollective.com
www.africanbookscollective.com

ISBN: 978-1-77934-041-2
EAN: 9781779340412

© Tendai Rinos Mwanaka 2024

DISCLAIMER
All views expressed in this publication are those of the author and
do not necessarily reflect the views of Mmap.

Table of Contents

3

4

Contributor's Bio Notes

Isaac Kilibwa is a lover of poetry from Kenya. His poems appear in Brittle Paper's 2023 Festive Anthology Vol. 2, Mystery Publishers' 2023 Strange Water anthology, Hawakal's 2023 Wives anthology and Mukana Press' much acclaimed 2022 Old Love Skin anthology. When not writing he teaches in Vihiga.

Clemency Madyangove is a Zimbabwean based Filmmaker who had worked on a number of film and television productions. Associate Producer of Gonarezhou the Movie, Best Narrative Film Pan African Film Festival (PAFF) USA. Script Developer and Producer of Poor Cousins Movie, Best Full Length Film National Arts Merit Awards (NAMA) Zimbabwe. Associate Producer Story of Nehanda Full Length Film (NAMA nomination). Producer and Story Developer of Solo and Mutsai Drama Series which broadcasted on NRTV-DSTV Zimbabwe. He is currently working on his first book "Up In Smoke" a memoir, which chronicles his life mistakes and misfortunes on the past decade.

Archie Swanson's first published poem appeared in 1973 in *English Alive,* an annual anthology of South African high school creative writing. The poem was also included in the 20 and 50-year *English Alive* commemorative anthologies. Poems have been published in the South African quarterly poetry magazines, *Stanzas* and *New Contrast* as well as the *Best New African Poetry Anthologies* (2015-2023), *Experimental Writing: Africa vs Latin America* (2017), *Experimental Writing: Africa vs Asia* — two poems in Japanese (2018), *Vol. 1,2 &3 of Africa vs North America* (2018, 2019 & 2022) and *Writing Robotics: Africa vs Asia* (2020), and Fixing Earth Africa, UK and

6

Ireland Writer's Anthology Vol.2 (2023). He has published four collections of poetry — *the stretching of my sky* (2018), *the shores of years* (2019), *beyond a distant edge* (2021) and *of clay* (2022). His fifth collection, *at the estuary* will be out in September 2024.

Ojonugwa John Attah is a Nigerian poet, educator, nature and street phone photographer, and book enthusiast. His writings and photography have been published online and in print in Nigeria, Kenya, and elsewhere. He is @OJohnAttah on X

Kimutai Kemboi Allan is a Kenyan writer residing in Nairobi. His works have been published or are forthcoming in the Redefining Poetry Anthology by Litterateur RW magazine, the "Best New African Poets 2023 Anthology", "Our Stories Redefined Anthology for African Writing 2023 (Poetry Edition)", The Piker Press, Prodigy Magazine, Our Poetry Archive, The INK Babies Literary Magazine, Written Tales, African Global Networks (AGN), Ake Review, The Active Muse, The Writer's Space Africa, The Kalahari Review, The Naluubale Review, Writers Resist and Havik's 2020 Anthology (Homeward). He is currently working on a Collection of Essays and an Anthology of Poems.

Catherine Awino is a poet from Kisumu, Kenya. She is 25 years old. She enjoys writing and has a certificate in Business Management from Kenya Institute of Management. Her poems are forthcoming in the Kalahari Review. When not writing she reads novels and articles. Catch her on Twitter here: @Catheri43385942

Kudakwashe Paul. Simbi saw the light of the earth on the 12th of May 1996 in Rusape . Simbi is an alumni from the University of Zimbabwe who studies B.A Honours Degree in English. He is a published author and poet. He contributed in quite a number of anthologies such as Speak, The Bleeding tree, Essential Voices, Pariah in Paradise, Bullfrog Vibrations: The Drumbeat, Zimbolicious Volume 7, Zimbolicious Volume 8, Voices Of Africa:

A Call For Freedom Anthology, Prima Anthology: Prose and Poetry From Africa Volume 1 just to mention a few.

Nyasha Celeste Makombe "Thee Poetic Raindrop" is a Zimbabwean phenomenal writer .Born October 13 1998   she fell in love with literature at a young age . Featured in 20 anthologies till date "Tesserae" , The Diary Of A Black Revolver" , "The Dawn of Valentine's Eve" to name a few. Her poems published in numerous newspapers namely "MT Kenya Times" , "The Midlands Observer" and "The Queensdale Report". Also "Lifestyle magazine" and "Intanga Poetry Corner". She is currently working on a solo poetry book and a novel. Her username is Celeste Makombe on facebook, Instagram and Twitter.

Martin Chrispine Juwa is a History teacher and Poet based in Lilongwe, Malawi. His poetry is a raw dialogue around identity, the natural environment, poverty and development, mental health, education, violence, spiritual healing and political activism. His work appears widely in both local and international online and print journals, magazines and anthologies including Southern Humanities Review, Held Magazine, The Poet Magazine, JAYL (Vol. 2), Orchards Journal, Project Muse, 4 BNAP Anthologies, Libero America Journal, Pensive Journal, Last Girls Club, Daily Drunk, Afreecan Read, Griots of Ubuntu, and many others. He has a debut poetry anthology titled *Drifting Smoke* (2020).

Oscar Gwiriri is a Zimbabwean published in more than 60 books, both fiction and text books. His two books *Hatiponi* and *Chitima nditakure* were NAMA awards nominees in 2019. He is a Certified Forensic Investigations Professional (CFIP) and a Certified Information Systems Security Professional (CISSP). He also holds a *Master of Science in Strategic Management Degree,   Bachelor of Business Administration, Associates of Arts in Business Administration, Diploma in Logistics and Transport (CILT, UK), Diploma in Workplace Safety and Health, Commanding United Nations Peacekeeping Operations Certificate,* and many other professional qualifications. He likes writing in his vernacular language (Shona) most.

Birungi Precious Uwineza is a female Ugandan, a passionate poetess, writer, public speaker, playwright and dancer. She has participated in the National Students Anti-corruption Challenge (2022-2023) and won a certificate. She has also involved herself in multiple debates at school. She has also written numerous poems though not featured in magazines but have been used by the writers club at her school. She has also involved herself in fighting corruption with IGG and has had an interview regarding the various forms of corruption. She has also written a number of stories on the Wattpad app. Due to her writing skills, she managed to become the chair person and editor of the writers club at her school (2021 - 2023). Currently she's in senior five at good hope Divine secondary school and she is the current Chief Judge of the school court and the Vice Chairperson and treasurer of the writers club. She has also participated in some debates at school as well as quizzes and speech writing competitions in school

Rogers Atukunda: I am a journalist, filmmaker, writer, and educator. My poem "Delilah" appeared in A Thousand Voices Rising: An Anthology of Contemporary African Poetry; "The Debase" in Praxis Magazine Online; "Beyond Beauty" in *Best New African Poets 2015 Anthology* and "Mama Millipede" in *Africanization and Americanisation Anthology, Volume 1*: Africa Vs North America. My short story "Daniela" was published in An Anthology of Contemporary Short Stories and Poems from East Africa. My essays "Unschooling the African to Deschool Society" and "On Footpath with Long Eye of History" were published in *Africanization and Americanisation Anthology, Volume 1: Africa Vs North America*. My critical paper: "Swallowing a Bitter Pill; The Subtext in Kihura Nkuba's When the African Wakes" was published on Acsademia.edu.

Mutiu Odetunde is a Nigerian poet and visual artist. He was born in the '80s in Lagos, Nigeria's erstwhile capital city. His artistic offerings (poetry and paintings) portray realities and happenings as they affect humans and the environment. He uses his creative abilities as a tool for raising positive awareness. He is a member of the Society of Nigerian Artists, SNA.

Mathews Mhango, by day, tackles financial puzzles as an internal auditor for the Malawian public sector. By night, his passion ignites as a poet, weaving words into narratives that have found a home in both local newspapers and international poetry anthologies.

Bunguswa Brian is a Kenyan literature scholar; a graduate of literature and linguistics, with great passion for poetry. He scripts and trains verses for Kenya music and drama festivals. Bunguswa has contributed in several continental and global poetry anthologies. Currently, he is a student of the Indian-based ALISON COLLEGE, undertaking a diploma in TEFL, Teaching English as a foreign language. He is also a teacher English at sunlight international schools.

Abdullatif Khalid, Latif The Sacred Poet is a male Ugandan passionate award-winning poet, educator, writer, word crosser, scriptwriter, essayist, content creator, orator, mentor, public speaker, hip-hop rapper, creative writing coach, and spoken word artist. He offers creative writing services and performs at projects focused on brand/ campaign awareness, luncheons, cooperate dinners, date nights, product launches, and concerts he is the founder of THE SACRED POETRY FIRM helps young creatives develop their talents and skills. His poems have been featured in several poetry publications, anthologies, journals, and magazines to mention but a few; *Best New African Poets 2022 Anthology, Writing Woman Anthology*....

Christopher Kudyahakudadirwe is a Zimbabwean who recently published a collection of short stories entitled *The Big Noise and Other Noises*. His poems appear in an anthology entitled *Harvest:*

The University of the Western Cape Masters in Creative Writing Poetry Anthology 2016 and in various magazines in and outside South Africa. He is currently working on a novel entitled Next to Nothing as part of his thesis in creative writing.

Adelmar Ramírez (México): Estudió una licenciatura en psicología y una maestría en escritura creativa en la Universidad de Texas en El Paso. Se doctoró en literatura y lenguas hispánicas por la Universidad de California Los Ángeles. Ha publicado los libros *Fuera de temporada* y *Prestanombres*. Apareció en la antología de poesía joven mexicana *Poetas parricidas: generación entre siglos*. Fue finalista de los premios Fundación Loewe y Juan Ramón Jiménez, y ganador del primer premio Transoceánico de poesía en honor a Claudia Lars. Se desempeñó como catalogador del archivo del genocidio guatemalteco para la Fundación Shoah (USC). Es profesor en Hood College.

Luis Ignacio Cárdenas (Venezuela): Diseñador gráfico, Ilustrador y editor. Lic. En educación mención: Lengua y Literatura (UNICA). Perteneció al colectivo literario y audiovisual PALABRACERA. Trabajó como diseñador y diagramador en la fundación Editorial Escuela El Perro y la Rana – Capitulo Zulia. Es editor en Ediciones Azalea y trabaja como editor audiovisual en la productora cinematográfica FOCO CREATIVO. Autor de los poemarios *Varios arrebatos* 2012 y *Un amor de color galaxia debajo de un amanecer agridulce* 2013 publicado por el Movimiento Poético de Maracaibo. Algunos de sus poemas han sido publicados en revistas literarias fuera y dentro del país. Incansable promotor de la lectura en escuelas, comunidades, cárceles y otros espacios.

Chaco de la Pitoreta (Honduras): Febrero de 1976, Manto, departamento de Olancho, Honduras. Abogado, defensor de Derechos Humanos, poeta, fotógrafo y trabajador cultural. Creador y fundador del *Colectivo Cultural Atrapados en Azul* y del Encuentro Internacional de *poetas de la Espera Infinita*. Propietario del sello *AteA-*

editorial y productor de los programas virtuales *"Desde El Acantilado"* y del proyecto de *biblioteca itinerante 7686) Nómadas en YouTube"*. Columnista en la revista internacional *Latino Rebels*, bloguero en *Radio Progreso y Equipo de Reflexión, Investigación y comunicación de la Compañía de Jesús*. Traducido, parcialmente, a **varios idiomas**, entre *ellos inglés, portugués, italiano, bengalí, polaco*. Actualmente es el *Jefe de la Casa de la Cultura y Museo de El Progreso*.

Nelson Roque Pereira (Ciego de Ávila, Cuba): Poeta e Investigador histórico; pertenece a la Organización internacional POETAP y a ELILUC; premiado en concursos, su obra ha sido publicada en varios medios, Libro Internacional Puente de palabras XIII 2016 Argentina; en Antología mundial Poetas siglo veintiuno, España; El abrazo del Nogal de Daimuz, antología Lorquiana tomo II, España; Ágora de la poesía, España; Alhucema Revista Internacional de Teatro y Literatura 2019, España; en varias antologías foráneas y en páginas Web de Cuba y del extranjero y en su poemario "Por los cauces de la noche", España, 2020.

José Carlos Monroy Rodríguez (México): Poeta y traductor náhuatl-español. Su obra ha sido publicada en medios físicos y digitales como *Sinfín, El círculo de poesía, La ciudad de los poemas* e *In xochitl, in cuicatl*, entre otros. Como traductor destacan sus trabajos como operador bilingüe náhuatl-españok para Telefónica México, la Secretaría de Desarrollo Rural y Equidad para las Comunidades de la Ciudad de México, el Gobierno Municipal de Tecámac y el concurso de traducción 1x1 del Periódico de Poesía de la Universidad Nacional Autónoma de México

Felicitas Casillo es profesora e investigadora en la Facultad de Comunicación de la Universidad Austral de la Argentina. Su programa de investigación se relaciona con temas vinculados a la hermenéutica del texto. Ha publicado los poemarios *El gran enero* (Del Dock, 2017), *El contorno del roble* (Rialp, 2020), y el libro *El* *discurso de la cultura: metáforas y caracterizaciones. El patrimonio en el caso del Teatro Colón* (Universidad Austral Ediciones, 2022).

Natalia Gómez (Campeche, México): Comunicóloga y docente. Beneficiaria del programa Jóvenes Creadores del Sistema de Apoyos a la Creación y Proyectos Culturales (SACPC) 2023, PECDA 2020 en Campeche y del Festival Interfaz ISSSTE 2017 en Yucatán. Ha participado en antologías como Anuario bilingüe de Poesía de San Diego y Novísimas, reunión de poetas mexicanas Vol. II. Algunos de sus textos se encuentran en revistas como Periódico de poesía, Círculo de Poesía, Punto en línea, Revista Altazor, Santa Rabia Magazine, The Ofi Press Magazine y Beltway Poetry. Actualmente es miembro del Proyecto de Escuela de Escritores Campechanos (ESCESCAM).

Okolo Chinua is a writer who writes for many reasons, the beauty of tomorrow being the foremost. Currently, he lives and writes from the suburbs of Onitsha, Anambra State, Nigeria.

David Chasumba is a Zimbabwean Writer and Poet. He has published two short story collections with Carnelian Heart Publishing: NAMA award winning, *The Mad Man on First Street and Other Short Stories (2022)* and *Behind the Façade and Other Stories (2024)*. David's poems have been published by Kalahari Review, Ipikai Poetry Journal, British Haiku Society anthology (2023) and in Best "New" African Poets (2023) anthology. David lives in Bexhill-on-sea, East Sussex, UK. X: @davidchasumba22

Lucas Zulu lives in South Africa, eMalahleni, Mpumalanga Province. He writes in Zulu and English and Nǀuu. His works is widely published in Asia, Africa, North America and Europe.

Adut Loi Akok is a south Sudanese poet, spoken word artist and an author of a poetry chapbook entitled " The Beauty Within Us " His work featured on Kalahari Review, Plot creatives magazine, Konch magazine, and best new African poets anthology (BNAP 2022). Adut Loi is the 2022-2023 second poetry winner of the national art competition sponsored by UNFPA in collaboration with shebab le shebab.

Introduction

After covering women issues in the anthology, *Writing Woman, An anthology of African and Asian writers, Vol 3*, which we issued in three parts, we felt we also needed to focus on Men's issues, considering Men are always left out on discourses to do with gender studies, or are always problematicised.

And this continual bashing of men has limited men's ability to express their thoughts and feelings on issues to do with these studies or just made them into submissive men, who are afraid of disagreeing with women on issues to do with gender.

And this is what I even experienced as I tried to promote this call. With quiet a number still feeling we should only focus on woman issues, saying men are still advantaged by the system. The danger is thinking that just because some men are advantaged it means every men is advantaged, and also thinking gender issues are to do with being a male or woman only. Yet for a lot of people, it's about class.

Some woman whom I invited to submit felt only males should contribute to this issue. But, I believe, there is no such thing as woman issues without men being involved. So I had to hold this line. All sexes were open to submit. And I realize submissions were fewer in this anthology than in the previous one for women, precisely because women felt they had nothing to contribute to an anthology on men, yet men don't feel the same way when it comes to women issues. And if we think this is a good way to solve these issues, we might as well end up like two people trying to talk to each other on a broken phone. One shouts to the other and that other shouts back, but no one hears the other.

I believe humans have to meet at an open platform where each person is allowed to express their own opinions and each person listens and try to understand what the other person is saying, thus these cross continental anthologies always tries to give such space to writers. Here are the areas we thought we could cover:

1. Man and home
2. man and education
3. man and workplace
4. man's rights
5. modern males struggles
6. man as figurehead
7. man and the economy
8. man and violence

Previous Anthologies in this series of African writers and Latin American Writers are *Experimental Writing, Africa vs Latin America Anthology Vol 1* and *Writing Grandmothers, Africa Vs Latin America Vol 2*. In this anthology, *Men: An International Anthology of African and Latin American writers Vol 3*, we have 29 writers plying their trade in Africa and Latin American regions and their diasporas, writing in English and Spanish. There are 50 poems, and 7 prose pieces(essays and fictions) from writers from these countries, Zimbabwe, South Africa, Malawi, Uganda, Nigeria, South Sudan, Mexico, Honduras, Venezuela, Cuba, Argentina and Kenya transacting around issues to do with modern man's rights and struggles.

15

A virgin at Forty
Alexander Khamala Opicho,

This is a song about love
that took place some years ago,
as a love-hate duel
Between Kharunda girl
And an African ogre,
Kharunda girl hailing then
Along the banks of river Maziwa
She had stubbornly refused
All offers for marriage,
from the local Kharunda boys,
Both rich and poor
tall and short, weak or strong,

Ugly and comely in the eye,
the girl had refused and
Sternly refused the treats for love,
she was disciplined to her callous
Pursuit of her cosmetic dream
to marry a mysterious, fantastic,
Lively, original and extra-ordinary man,
no other woman in history
Of human marriage ever married,

Her name was Goodhamlet Lovehill,
Daughter of a peasant, from the Nyungu -shire
Her foremen (in)famous for poverty in pottery
And still now hustled often
For food, clothing, and other calls
That make one an ordinary Kharunda ,
She grew up without a local boy friend,
Anywhere in the Kharunda world,
Lo! She was the first English girl to knock
The age of forty five while a virgin,
she never got deflowered
In her teens as other Kharunda girls
she preserved her purse
With maximal carefulness
In her wait for a black man,
her father, of course a peasant,
His trade was a waver between
Ancestral legacy of miserable pot making
To barber surgery and horse shearer,
he often asked her what she wants
In life before her marriage,

Which man she really wanted,
her specification was an open
Eyesore to her father-
No blinkers could save the father's pale
for she wanted a black tall man,
Strong and ruggedly dark in the skin,
And he must actively own a kingdom.
Fables taken to her from Africa
Were that such an African man
was only one but none else,
His glorious name was;
Akhatembete kho bwibo khakhalikha no bwoya,
When the Kharunda girl heard the chimerical
In the name of her potential husband,
She felt a super bliss in her spine;
she yearned for the day of rendezvous,
She crashed into desperate burning for true love
With a man having wonderful name like
Akhatembete kho bwibo khakhalikha no bwoya.

Rumours of this girl's despair
And dilemma for love reached Africa,
But in the wrong ears,
not in the human ears,
Unfortunately the ears of the ogres,
Seasoned in the evil art of power and love,
the rumour was received and treated
As classified information among the African ogres,
They guarded it not to leak
To African humans at all at all
lest humans enjoy their human status
to enjoy most love in the offing

From the English girl,
they thus swiftly plotted a ploy
to lure and win the virgin
from royal land;
Kharunda-land.

Firstly,
The African ogres recruited one of their own
the most handsome middle aged male ogre,
More handsome than all in humanity,
And of course African ogres are beautiful
And handsome than African humans, no match,
the ogres are more gifted in stature,
Physique, eugenics and general overtures
they always outplay African humans
On matters of intelligence, they are shrewder;
Ogres are aggressive and swashbuckling in manners;
Fear is none of their domain
Craft and slyness is their breakfast,
super is the result; success, whether pyrrhic or Byronic,
Is their sweetest dish,
they then schemed to get the girl at whatever cost,
they made a move to name one of their own;
Akhatembete khobwibo khakhalikha no bwoya,
viciously naming one of their handsome
Middle-aged ogre with this name.

Then they set off on foot,
From Congo in the heart of Africa
Moving to the north towards the target
Where Kharunda land sleeps like a virgin
Where the beautiful girl of the times,

19

Goodhamlet Lovehill hail,
they were three of them,
Walking funnily in cyclopic steps
Of young male African ogres,
keeping themselves humorously high
By feigning how they will dupe the girl,
how they will slyly decoy potter's daughter
a village pumpkin of the girl
In to their trap for show of their mighty
and effortlessly make her walk on foot
to Africa, in pursuit of love
on this muse and sweet wistfulness
They broke out into loud gewgaws of laughter,
In such emotional bliss they now jump up wildly
Forgetting about their tails
they initially stuffed inside white long trousers,
The tails now wag and flag crazily;
Feats of such wild emotions gave the ogres
Superhuman synergy to walk *cyclopically*,
a couple of their strides made them to cross Uganda,
Kenya, Somali, Ethiopia and Egypt
just but in few days, as sometimes they ran
In violent stampedes on fire of wile love
Singing in a cryptic language
the funny ogres songs;

Dada wu ndolelee!
Dada wu ndolelee!
Kuyuni kwa mnja
Sa kwingile khundilila!

Ehe kuyuni Mulie!

20

Ehe kuyuni mulie!
Omukhana oyo
Kaloba khuja lilia!

They then laughed loudly,
Farted cacophonously and
Jumped wildly, as if possessed,
they used happiness and
Raucous joy as a strategy
To walk miles and miles
which you are to cover
When moving on foot from Congo
To Kharunda land where God's eye
never blink , waver or flab in a flap
they finally crossed Morocco and
Walked into Khurunada-land ,
They by-passed sleeping lands
Walking piecemeal
into native land
Of the beautiful girl,

the three ogres reached well ,
Though they were all surprised
every woman and man there was leperous ;
People there walked slowly lest hit wounds
they made minimum noise from sick voice
No shouting publicly whatsoever,
a stark contrast to human behaviour
And ogre culture in Africa; very rambunctious,
before they acclimatized to disorderly life
 an over-sighted upset befell them
Piling and piling menace of pressure to piss,

21

Gripped all the three ogre brothers the same time,
None of them had knowledge of public utilities,
They all wanted to micturate openly
Had it not been being shy and nervous
                    Of the slender and tall beautiful girls
                    ceaselessly thronging the streets,

                    they persevered and moved on
              In expectation of coming to the end,
                    Out-skirt of the strange town
                    So that they can get a woodlot,
                    from where they could hide behind
                    To do open defecation
                    all was in vain; they never came
                    to any end of the town,
              Neither did they come by a tumbled-down house
              No cul-de-sac was in sight, only endless highway,
              Sandwiched between tall skyscraping buildings,
        One of the ogres came up with an idea, to drip the piss
        Drop by drop in their panties, as they walk to their destiny,
        They all laughed but not loudly, in controlled giggles
                    And executed the idea minus haste.

              They finally came down to the banks of river Maziwa ,
                    Identified the home of Goodhamlet Lovehill
              The home had neither main gate nor metallic doors,
              They entered the home walking in humble majesty,
                    Typical of racketeering ogre, in a swindling act,
              The home was silent, no one in sight to talk to
              The ogres nudged one another, repressing the mirth,
                    Hunchbacked lass surfaced, suddenly materialized
              Looking with a sparkle in the eye, talking pristine tongue,

, Her words were as piffling
as speech of a mad woman at the fish market,
Ogres looked at her in askance.

An ogre with the name;
Akhatembete khobwibo khakhalikha nobwoya
Opened its sorcerous mouth to talk
Voodoo secret planted under its tongue
As love charms to conjure and beguile the girl
Into injured judgment for blind love,
It asked the girl where could be the latrine pits,
for micturation only but no any other long business
The hunchbacked lass gave them a direction
to the toilets inside the house,
She did it in a full dint of English elegance and gentility,
But all the ogres were discombobulated to the peak
about the latrine pit inside the house,
they all went into the toilet at the same time,
to the chagrin of the hunchbacked lass
she had never seen such in her land
she struggled with a chuckle alot
to repress her mirth
as the Kharundas
never get amused
at folly.

It is a tradition among the ogres to fart,
Whenever they are pissing in the African bush,
But now the ogres are in a fix, a beautiful fix of their life
If at all they fart, the flatulent cacophony will be heard outside
By the curious eavesdroppers under the eaves of the house,
They murmured among themselves to tighten their anal muscles

So that they can micturate without usual African accomplice; the
tweeee!
All succeeded to manage, other than Akhatembete khobwibo
khakhalikha nobwoya, urinating but with a low tziiiiiiii sound
from his anus, they didn't laugh,
Ogres walked out of privities relaxed
like a catholic faithful swallowing a Eucharist sacrament,
The hunchback girl ushered them
to where they were to sit in the common room
They all sat with air of calm on their face,
Akhatembete Khobwibo khakhalikha no bwoya
led the conversation, by announcing to the girl
that he is Lovehill's visitor from Africa,
To which the girl responded with caution
that lovehill is at the barbershop,
Giving hand to her father
in shearing the horses,
and thus she is busy,
No one is allowed to meet her,
at that particular hour of the day
But he pleaded to the hunchback girl
only to pass tidings to Lovehill,
That Akhatembete Khobwibo khakhalikha no bwoya
from Africa has arrived and he is yearning to meet her,
The girl went bananas on hearing the name
The hunch on her back visibly shook,
Is like she had heard the name often,
She then became prudent in her senses,
And asked the visitor not to make anything—
Near a cat's paw out of her person,
She implored the visitor to confirm
if at all he was what he was saying

to which he confirmed in affirmation,
then she went out swiftly
like a tail of the snake,
to pass tidings
to her sister
Lovehill.

She went out shouting her sister's name,
A rare case to happen in Nyungu-shire,
One to make noise in the broad day light,
With no permission from the local leadership,
She called and ululated Lovehill's name
For her to hear from wherever she was,
Of which she heard and responded;
what is the matter my dear little sister?
What ails you?
Akhatembete Khobwibo khakhalikha no bwoya is around!
She responded back in voice disturbed by emotional uproar,
what! My sister why do you cheat me in such a day time?
Am not cheating you my sister, he is around in our father's house,
Is he? Have you given him a drink, a sweet wine of our land ?
My sister I have not, I feared that I may mess up your visitors
With my hunched shoulders, I feared sister, forbid,
Ok, I am coming, running there, tell him to be patient,
Let me tell him sister just right now,
And make sure you come before his patience is stretched.

Lovehill almost went berserk
On getting this good tidings
about the watershed presence,
Of the long awaited suitor,

her face exploded into vivacity,
Her heart palpitating on imagination of
finally getting the husband,
She went out of the barber shop
running and ululating,
Leaving her father behind,
confounded and agape,
She came running
towards her father's main house
Where the suitor is sited,
with the chaperons,
She came kicking
her father's animals to death,
Harvesting each and every fruit, for the suitor,
She did marvel before she reached
where the suitor was;
Harvested ten bananas,
mangoes and avocadoes,
Plums, pepper,
watermelons, lemons and oranges,
She kicked dead five chicken,
five goats, rams,
Swine, rabbits, rats,
pigeons and hornbills,

When she reached the house,
she inquired to know,
who among them could be the one;
Akhatembete Khobwibo Khakhalikha no bwoya,
But her vocals were not guttural enough,
She instead asked who among you

is *a key tempter go weevil car no lawyer?*
The decoy ogre promptly responded;
here I am the queen of my heart as he stood up,
she took the ogre into her arms, whining,
babie! Babie, babie, come!
She carried the ogre swiftly in her arms,
To her tidy bed room,
she placed the ogre on her bed,
Kissed it and then they kissed one another
At a rate of hundred or more kisses per a minute,
The kissing sent both of them crazy,
But spiritual craft gave the ogre a boon
To maintain some sobriety,
Lo! Libido of virginity held Lovehill
In boon-less state of sexual feat,
Defenseless and impaired in judgment
it extremely beclouded her judgment;
She removed and pulled of their clothes,
libidinous feat blurring her sight
From seeing the scarlet tail projecting
From between the buttocks of the ogre,
a clean and clear vestige of bestiality,
she forcefully took the ogre into her arms,
Putting the ogre between her legs,
the ogre's uncircumcised penis went erect,
It effectively penetrated the virgin's purse,
the ogre broke virginity of Lovehill,
Making her to feel maximum warmth of pleasure
as it released its germinal seed into her body,
Ecstasy gripped her until she fainted;
the ogre erected more on its first ejaculation;

Its penis became more stiff and sharp;
it never pulled out its penis
From the now warm and swollen purse ,
Instead it introduced further deeper and deeper
Into her uterus, reaching the
Virgin depth inside her with gusto,
she screamed, wailed, farted, scratched,
threw her neck, kissed crazily and pissed,
On the rhythms of the ogre's waist gyrations,
it was maximum pleasure ,
She reached her second orgasm before the ogre;
it took further one hour before releasing,
she was beaten; she thought she was not in in heaven
not in her father's house
She thought she was in Timbuktu
riding on a mosquito to Eldorado,
Where she could not be found by her father whatsoever,
The ogre pulled her up, helped her to dress up,
She begged that they go back to the common room,
Lest her father finds them here, he would quarrel,
They went back to the common room,
Found her father talking to other two ogres,
She shouted to her father before anyone else,
That 'father I have been showing him around our house, '
'He has fallen in love with our house; he is passionate about it, '
Akhatembete khobwibo khakhalikha nobwoya was shy,
He greeted the father and resumed his chair, with wryly dignity.

An impromptu festival took place,
Fully funded by the father ,
There was meat of all type from pork to chicken,
Greens were also there in plenty, pepper and watermelons,

Lovehill's mother remembered to prepare tripe of a goat
For the key visitant who was the suitor; Akhatembete,
Food was laid before the ogres to enjoy themselves,
As all others went to the other house for a brainstorming session,
But the hunch-backed girl hid herself behind the door,
To admire the food which visitors were devouring,
As she also spied on the table manners
of the visitors, for stories to be shared later ,
Perhaps between herself and her mother,
when visitors will be gone,
Some sub-human manners unfolded to her as she spied,
One of the ogres swallowed a spoon and a table fork,
Again Akhatembete khobwibo khakhalikha no bwoya,
Uncontrollably unstuffed his scarlet tail from the trouser,
The chill crawled up the spine of hunchbacked girl,
She almost shouted from her hideout, but she restrained herself,
She swore to herself to tell her father that the visitors are not humans
They are superhuman, Tarzans or mermaids or the werewolves,
The ogre who swallowed the spoon remorsefully tried to puke it back,
Lest the hosts discover the missing spoon and cause brouhaha,
It was difficult to puke out the spoon;
 it had already flowed into the stomach,

Lovehill, her father, her mother and her friend Najilonte,
Najilonte the girl from the neighborhood,
Lovehill had fished, to work for her as a best maid,
 as a chaperon, all went back to the house
 Where the ogres had already finished eating,
they found ogres sitting idle squirming

and flitting in the spongy chairs
As if no food had ever been presented to them in a short while ago,
One ogre even shamelessly yawned, blinking his eyes like a snake,
They all forgot to say thanks for the food, no thanks for lunch,
But instead Akhatembete announced on behalf of other ogres,
That they should be allowed to go as they are late for something,
A behaviour so sub-human, given they were new suitors ,
the father was uneasy, was irritated but he had no otherwise,
For he was desperate to have his daughter get married,
He had nothing to say but only to ask his daughter,
If she was going right-away with her suitor or not,
To which she violently answered yes I am going with him,
the mother kept mum only shooting miserable glances
From one corner of the house to another, to the ogres also,
She totally said nothing, as Lovehill was predictably violent
To any gainsayer in relation to her occasion of the moment,
the father wished them all well in their life,
And permitted her to go and have good life,
With Akhatembete, her suitor she had yearned for with equanimity,
she was so confused with joy; her day of marriage is beholden,
She hurriedly packed up as if being chased by a monster,
she forgot to put on her panty, nor did she remember to carry one,
she only fixed her chaplet and felt herself very ready for the
journey,
The ogres went away with Goodhamlet Lovehill and Najilonte,
The hunchbacked girl followed them crying,
wailing to come along with them,
She decried loneliness that would torture her,
in the absence of her sister.

The hunch-backed girl persistently cried, following her sister,

Begging and begging to come along with her sister,
Lovehill often chased her to go back home,
An act to which the ogres Reacted negatively,
Akhatembete on every turn cautioned Lovehill
Not to chase her, but to leave the girl alone,
To come along and travel with them,
She disdained the idea,
As the hunch on back of the girl
will only make her a public laughing stock,
As for sure,
Who in the world,
of entire humanity,
Ever got married
along with a hunchback sibling?
The hunch-back hid herself
behind the bush, and totted them,
Lovehill and the ogres walked
for kilometers and even forgot
About the hunchback,
thinking the hunchback had returned home
Only for the hunchback to surface
After they had covered seventy five miles,
She announced her presence by
suddenly wailing from behind,
All of them were agog,
on looking back to find the girl,
the hunch protuberating on back
like a tor on the Mountain,
Then it was the time
Akhatembete as the key person,
Domineered the situation,

he commanded the hunchback,
to come and walk with them,
as other ogres laughed themselves to tears
Lovehill frowning in shame,
while Najilonte counseled her not to mind,

Tell us your name our dear little sister?
Demanded one of the ogres,
teasing the hunchback to tell them her name,
Of which they were ready to giggle,
my name is Nellykeen,
The ogres giggled, mocking
the sound of the name,
as it makes no sense in their African
language of the ogres,
what hogwash of a name!
The hunchback chickened
and apologized
for having a silly name,
In the usual manners of the civilized
when faced with defeat,
One of the ogres shouted rudely;
What you have told us is human nonsense!
It is utter rubbish from a useless wonk!
I have to give you a name now!
Your name from now hence forth is Nakitumba!
Meaning the hunchbacked one,
this is how we call the hunchbacks
In our community of Babukusu,
We are the *Ba*bukusu for your information,

Do you get me you dear little girl?
We are found in Africa, in east Africa;
Congo, Uganda, Sudan, Kenya, Ethiopia,
Somalia, Rwanda and Burundi,
You the hunchbacked ones don't come from God,
You are the off-cuts from leisure of the devil;
you are harbingers of bad luck,
Do you get me Madam Nakitumba?
You shrewd daughter from land of leprosy ,
Nakitumba responded in maximum obsequiety
Yes I do my brother-in-law,
but above all I am thankful
For the wonderful name,
And also for permitting me to come,
with you to your country of adventure,
For my break from mundane factories,
Two ogres apart from Akhatembete
Broke into loud cackles,
Chanting the new name;

Nakitumba! Nakitumba!
Nakitumba! Nakitumba!
Mulamwa Nakitumba!
Kene khukhwirire
Ekhafu ewunwa
Mala! Oliemo kamaneke!

They chanted jumping around,
from one side to another,
Throwing their hands in the air,
they then laughed and giggled
Until they all fell down

33

In the sand dunes of Morocco,
As Akhatembete,
Lovehill and Najilonte smiled,
Restraining their laughers,

They reached home in Congo,
in the thicket of bantu forest,
Each ogre carrying a girl
in fact shoulder high or on the back,
As the girls had gotten defeated
 from walking somewhere in Sudan,
Akhatembete carrying Victoria
in a style connoting some slyness,
One ogre carrying Nakitumba,
its hand gripping Nakitumba's hunch
the ogre that had carried Najilonte
Was panting with sound, it was exhausted,
during this porterage is when Akhatembete
 Discovered something funny;
Lovehill did not have her under panties on,
she was naked with no undergarments,
He felt her by his fingers, but he didn't announce,
He felt the warmth of her thighs in silence,
He was in this gusto for a long time,
None of the others ogres discovered Akhetembete's fortune
Until they finally entered their home of the ogres,
Hoards of ogres came running,
To receive their brothers back home,
All of them were naked, both female and male,
Tails wagging high in the air, a symbol of joy
Akhatembete and other ogres went jubilant,
They all now put down the girls,

Threw away their make-believe clothes
And remained naked to their nudity,
As it is an abomination to put on clothes,
In the world of the ogres,
All ogres were now in a song and a dance,
Akhatembete khobwibo khakhalikha nobwoya,
The top dancer, his tail wagging the most,
the girls were surprised,
They realized that they were now in the jaws of hyena,
they began crying, in confirmation of their goof,
But Nakitumba joined the ogre dancers,
the hunch on her back tilting rapidly,
From which the ogres found a lot of theatre,
they sang, danced, laughed and teased,
Old female ogres with one eye also came out to dance,
with pipes on their mouth,
Some challenged Nakitumba to a dance competition;
some just shook their shoulders,
In a stupid style, as they whetted their appetite
for a human meat, a foreign meat,
A dish they had never had in their lives
as a community of cannibals.

the girls somberly sat,
desperately looking on, as ogres bargained,
on whether to eat them straight-away or not,
ogres charged with role of community butcherers
Came in wielding their tools of work,
an opportunity to slaughter a human being,
instant violence broke out among the teenaged ogres,
fighting one another in a deathly attacks,
Fighting over the right to eat the vulvas,

A war that was stopped by an elderly female ogre
Coming out to caution unschooled juvenile ogres
By warning that vulvas are never eaten by children,
they are only eaten by married male ogres,
As an amulet to boost sexual capability,
the truce resumed, then a song and a dance again,
Ogres were in the carnival,
when the noise stopped the,
elderly male ogre purely naked, stood up,
to address the community over the matter of time;
eating their new victuals,
the three girls
from the servile land ,
his balls were pronouncedly hanging,
he danced for some time
as his balls perambulated,
then coughed loudly,
a way of clearing his voice for a brief speech;
he yelled;

heberirikwei hei hewunooo!
Response from the rest;
he e wunooo!
Heberirikwei hei hewunooo!
Hewuonooo!
Bakhana bali ano!
Haaaaaaaaaa!
Balinka enyanke!
Enyanke yajaaa!
Khayo ve munye!
Ve munye!
Khubalie mujuli!

Mujuli!
Khoroooooo!
Khoroooooo!

My dear brothers and all the leaders
Of our Babukusu ogre community,
In our tradition we don't eat tired preys,
Let them sleep, for their blood to flow in their veins,
So that when we eat them tomorrow,
They will be palatable, sweet to munch
Myself as an elder, I will have the hunch,
From the back of Nakitumba,
Not for eating but for voodoo,
That will protect our community
From all evil machinations.
All the ogres responded in one voice
Yeeeeees!
All ogres dispersed and they instructed Wenwa wa Ilungu,
The handsome ogre who impersonated to be the
Akhatembete khobwibo khakhalikha no bwoya,
To be the caretaker of the captives,
He took them to another hut,
terribly dirty, without a door,
Human skulls all over the floor,
And eerie psychopompous sounds,
Was irregularly heard in a faint timbre
A lot of wood hanging in the roof,
Possibly used as coal for boiling human carcass
He commanded them to sleep, on the skulls,
After saying we are the ones, who ate their bodies,
Above there is the fire wood we used to boil them,
the girls were wordless,

But Nakitumba was jovial teasing the ogres on the way,
Then darkness fell and they were to sleep, and they slept,
All other ogres went for a beer taking spree, bound to end at dawn,
In preparation for tomorrow, they left the compound dead silent,
Apart from Wenwa on the sentry, who was deep a sleep,
Snoring like a toad emitting a call for love,
or like an old train
Passing by the infamous station Sudi
in Bungoma county of Kenya,

Nakitumba developed a trick for them to escape;
she began whining in deep soprano
Very and sharply irritating voice,
The syncopations nothing else but call for empathy,
Like that one of a very sick person, in deep pain,
About to die in an hour's time,
When the ogre on the sentry heard it,
He woke up quarrelling violently,
Why all the stupid noise?
Nakitumba responded artfully,
in a low melodious voice;
My dear brother-in-law, I am very sick,
Am feeling deep pains in the hunch,
On my back, I will die if not assisted,
My medicine is simple, very simple,
Just water from any Lake around here

But it must be in a basket made of reeds
Or on a handmade papyrus platter,
I will be ok; the platter must be a basket-like,
Please do me a favour the way I did you,

to call a girl for you when you came to England,
Kindly help me, I will appreciate.

The ogre felt it,
Not that he was taken by Nakitumba's prayer,
But because an elderly ogre
Had earmarked Nakitumba's hunch,
if she will be found dead
The community will blame the sentry keeper,
As the ogres don't eat rotting carcass,
They only eat what they have slaughtered,
He opted to go for the waters, from Lake Sango,

Akhatembete calculated he could only take three hours,
To cover a thousand miles,
From Congo to Lake Sango, to and fro,
Given his cyclopic strides of the ogre,
He commanded Nakitumba to be silent
As he will be back soon,
with waters from the lake on
The basket-work of a platter,
Then he flew away,
his footsteps causing some tremors,
When they died off, there was silence and calm,
Then Nakitumba knew that he is now far away,
The safest time to escape and run away,
She woke up the two girls;
And whispered to them; it is safe
Let us run away,
The three girls hopelessly accepted
she commanded them not to carry anything,
that belonged to the ogres

39

But to carry all else that theirs,
the only sure way to forestall,
Revanchistic voodoo,
they escaped off walking,
No need for running
as commanded by Nakitumba,
notwithstanding fear,
that domineered
They were sobbing;
shedding tears grievously,
Without further hope,
They walked and walked,
In the darkness of African night
Three girls in the moonless night,
Walking the hinterland of Africa,
When dawn came they were lucky
To see the morning star in the east,
they thought that it was an ogre
Looking at them from the sky,
Najilonte confirmed to them
that it was an ogre,
But no,
It was one of the planetary objects,
Usually visible during the early morning,
when viewed from Africa,
Lovehill was tired; she wanted to lie down die,
or even better to be eaten by an African ogre,
But Nakitumba challenged her to soldier on,
After a short while of silence and painstaking walking,
Very huge bull frog, the size of a Volkswagen car
Appeared in their front, leaping in a relaxed mode,
They wanted to run away, but Nakitumba said no,

Let us have a look-see of it, we don't need to be afraid,
To their surprise the frog addressed them ,
The frog introduced herself as a grandmother,
she claimed to be knowing avaricious stupidity of the ogres,
She told the girls not to fear, as she will get them back
To their home, away from man-eating ogres
the frog poured out all the contents of its stomach
Then she ordered the girls to jump into the empty stomach,
They jumped in without question, Najilonte first,
Then Lovehill and finally Nakitumba,
Then it swallowed back her stuffs
She had initially vomited, plus the filthy fluid,
then she began humping slowly towards Kharunda-land ,
She jumped for three decades before getting there,

When the ogres discovered that the girls had escaped,
All of them began to chase,
to hunt for them everywhere in Africa,
No girls was found,
they often met a huge frog,
with an extra swollen stomach,
The ogres, commanded the frog to puke whatever
that was making its stomach to swell abnormally,
but when the frog puked first the dirty fluid,
the fluid nauseated the ogres, the ogres were repulsed,
and told the frog not to spit more, but to lick back its puke
and walk away, of which the frog always politely complied,
The ogres became tired and gave up the hunt,
On their way back, ogres met the snake,
They asked it if it had seen the three girls,
One with a rump on her back,
Out of snobbish pride, the snake lied to the ogres,

41

That it saw the girls and killed all of them,
Even they are already putrefied due to its deathly poison,
The ogres flogged the snake,
Terribly that no other living creature,
Happened to die of as the snobbish snake
Did in the hands of the ogres,
Then the ogres declared it a loss,
Due to their folly
to which they surrendered and walked home,

Inside the stomach of the frog Lovehill was pregnant,
Pregnant for Wenwa,
Alias Akhatembete khobwibo khakhalikha no bwoya,
when the time neared for delivery
Her stomach bulged sideways,
Instead of protruding forward,
Nakitumba predicted the twins,
when time of delivery came,

the twins were safely born,
Peacefully without any medical trouble,
Nakitumba cut the umbilical cords,
Nakitumba placed the placentae in a position
in which they could be digested away by the frog,
the twin brothers grew up into lively babies,
apart from the sixth fingers and toes on the first twin,
Compensated by a charming birthmark on the face
and sexy gap in the front teeth of the second twin,
all of them in the stomach of the frog
Survived for decades on the diet of white ants

Which the frog swallowed piecemeal,
without chewing, each and every evening,
until the frog reached in Kharundalan,
It found Lovehill's mother sitting lonely,
On the sepulcher of her husband who had died a decade ago,
The frog surprised the old mother with spoken kharunda-speak,
the frog asked only for a permission to puke,
the old lady permitted the animal to puke,
the frog puked out its usual filthy entrails,
then Nakitumba, followed by Lovehill,
the twin brothers, then Najilonte,
Miracle and joy overwhelmed that entire home,
Lovehill begged her mother
that she wants to return back to Africa
To search for the father of her two sons,
But everyone refused, she also complied,
And stayed in Kharunda-land
She stayed and grew up
Only to become the Queen-mother
Her sons became the two Princes
The frog is kept unto now in home of old frogs
At Nyungushire menagerie of small animals,
Let my tale in this song die now
To let myself live forever
to sing more songs
Of tales like this one

A Picture of May
Isaac Kilibwa

On Twenty-sixth of Ninety-two afternoon
Jogoo Road is a gentle mirage
Kissed by a whisper of cold premonition.

I stand between the hands of squatting
Nuclides, a child of love,
They hold each other with steady stares
That bristle the rustling flowers on my head:
A cluster of lush black stigmata.

It must be Sunday for the church that
Glistens in my father's eyes when he winks
At the mechanical eye that whirrs in my ear
A song of free falling numbers. Almost
Like a clock's footsteps.

In his whorls, I feel my blood tsunami into coves and
Sheet along calloused contours. For a lifetime

We argue and fight about the dreams he makes me
Journey as I strive to claim a mountain of fog
As thick as cream and falls of demurring honey,

Like Caleb. I scream, give me this mountain.
We speak at length on the philosophy of lust and
Debate Bible verses.

When at last I find the ridges of a countryside
I think I find peace at a land beyond a bloody river

44

And when my sister leaves for work in Nairobi
As the last of an exodus, I stand between

Two bent parents once more unable to deem myself
Self-righteous enough to judge him.

Clothing
Isaac Kilibwa

There are words that fit only a husband,
Like you are my happy place.

I saw a man once strive his whole life
To save his wife

And when at last she was lost
He stood judgment for it.

A time comes with tired limbs when
You can't afford to utter words you don't mean

You can't work enough anymore
To please your own clothing.

And that is when sons old enough to have
Sons old enough to intuit that real gods

Are not infallible, turn and kick at that place
Where the udder is soft.

There are words that fit only a father,
Jesus is one.

Counting Stars

Isaac Kilibwa

A boy drifts through cloudy curtains
On the shoulders of a god
Counting stars.
A seer says that they step on your
Toes when they are young
And tread on your heart when old.

A man is an inheritance, the scribbling of a birth right
Are hieroglyphs that conjure to spell peace in so many tongues.
After he breaks a girl so irreparably he seeks
His father's help.
He weathers his judgment like a man for
No longer is he a boy from then.

You see him learn to make visits to morgues
And collect little speeches for epilogues and blurbs:
Make a hobby out of misery for he's now the tribe's orator.
You see him as an unwilling priest at funeral processions
And speaking things like, 'a Christian is a domino of deaths,'
You see him, with poems that are little regrets and repentances, no?

He stands on a boulder of family's goodwill and
Stares at a sea raging about him, bashing its head
Against the obsidian rocks that chip away like black tax -
Lawyers buffet in warships with cannons of disdain
And labels such as deadbeat, he walks away calm

But sobs in the skin of a moon-haunted dusk.

At last the stars of heaven glisten in a pool of tears
And a rote the children mime devours the night
In a voice of accusation, my father was a hyena.
But a man is an inheritance, a war against himself
And when in arthritis' grip you halt down the beach
Your bones sigh next to his and it's your turn to count.

Jake Vegas
Archie Swanson

a year later and he's grown slower still
added another 15 kilograms
a Marlon Brando look-alike
eyes slanted and heavily jowled
everything on him is black except the gypsy rings
wearing a Blues Brothers' hat he fronts the Black Diamonds band
he wears a shabby jacket

but shabby is not the way he sings
laying down the blues with well-oiled growl
he holds the mike within a giant paw
he occupies the stage with the charm of Al Capone
the band he fronts are tight as string
it's the blues they play
it's the blues he sings

summoned to the stage he's like a walrus lumbering
he has to catch his breath to mount the two-step stair
his lungs are heaving… he is sucking in the air
half a song delivered
and he sits down on the Marshall amp to rest
his smile is overlayed with the pain
that's written on his face

the crowd erupts each time he sings
his heart is large and failing
arthritis has him in its stranglehold
he sings authentic blues but he is looking old
I wonder just how long he has to go

ain't nothing but the blues he howls into the mic
this is the saga of big bad Jake

father time
Archie Swanson

the same each day at Coffee Time on York
the smile that greets all souls that wander in
it may be tea or coffee that they seek
perhaps a pie is what they're thinking of

or even cheesecake balanced on a fork
to follow tasty chicken ala king
but more than food he dishes up each week
it's happy repartee he brings with love

his voice not strong as it might once have been
his gait a little slowed… he's tall and thin
he's seen a lot of life… the hair is grey

this morning though he's nowhere to be seen
emergency response has been called in
and it's our turn to give some love today

epitaph
Archie Swanson

on this scuffed Cape Town day I have returned to grandad's grave
that has no pompous epitaph – just simple words that say
WALTER DONALD SWANSON   1903 – 1985   MUSICIAN
next to the modest granite plinth a hardy succulent has taken root
a better option than the UV-faded plastic blooms about

his mini bio has no words to say of the symphonies he wrote
nothing of his operettas performed in modest prep school halls
the hunched figure on the City Hall conductor's podium
the funerals and weddings that as organist he played
Gilbert and Sullivan rehearsed to perfection

and nothing of early morning bitter coffee
ladled spoon by spoon onto my tiny tongue
the year he came to stay… the year my Danish 'mormor' passed
away
who always gave me bread to feed the doves
that settled on her Sea Point balcony

Dear dad.
Kemistry

This is an open letter to you.

I'm writing to you, to let you know how the things you did, the things you said, the things you didn't do and didn't say and how they really broke me.

Dear dad.
I loved you so much, daily I waited for you to return from work, even when you returned late, i wanted to let you how much your boy was growing, but you were many things but a father wasn't part of them.

"I was eight when I cried to you,
My heart was breaking, my soul was torn
I couldn't control the sobs, the tears wouldn't cease,
As I told you how she made me sit on her knee, a painful release.
You said I'm a man, to shake it off, but inside, I'm breaking down.

I became toy, a pawn in a twisted game, even when I tried to scream, only silence came.

Dad I had to become a man when I was barely a child.
My tender shoulders got used to bills piling up.
All I had was the smiles plastered on my face, some mask I had gotten used to wearing.

You never bothered about the miles I had to go, you never had a smile waiting for me, when all you left me was just your last name, and the shoes I had gotten so used to wearing even as a toddler.

I craved your touch, your reassurance, but instead, I was met with silence, devoid of nurture."

But then I had to be a man.
I can't be seen as vulnerable, less I'm tagged a weakling.
I dare not cry, unless I'll be branded a sister.
I can't vent, I still have many fees hovering around my neck like generational curses.

So this letter is to let you know that I'm tired.
Tired of hiding behind lines, and tear filled pillows.
Tired of swallowing lumps of pains.
Tired of wearing scars that aren't healing.
I'm tired of the shoes I'm wearing.
I'm tired of dancing to the tune, you and everyone has played for me.
I'm tired of acting the script you all drafted.
Now I'm going back to being a child,before becoming a man.

I FELL IN LOVE WITH DYING

Ojonugwa John Attah

I fell in love with dying but she won't love me back
It left me broken in many places, into tiny bits like the tiny bits of
bodies found after an explosion
I have changed lovers like clothes;
First, there was loneliness, then anxiety, pills, insomnia, and then
depression
Loneliness is sometimes my middle name;
I want to be alone and away from every available pair of eyes
At night, insomnia creeps into my bed;
we make love all night and in the morning my eyes continue to
search for an elusive sleep.
The doctor's pills do not work – nothing works including solutions.
People tell me that men do not cry;
but I can show you every bowl that ever collected tears from my
eyes;
every pillow that retained my tears in the day and at night.
A silent storm rages inside of me but I cannot stop it;
how can I hold back angry waves when I am all alone beside the
beach?
I cannot speak about the storm that rages inside of me.
Someone once said to me: "We can all struggle; if we share how we
feel, the burden becomes less weightier. We can only sow healing
when we share our struggles."
In front of each one of us a mirror is held up; we choose what we
want others to see and this is where many of us hide the truth
Behind the smiles and the happy faces when the cameras flash in
our faces, many cry themselves to sleep
I have recently fallen in love with books; the smell from a multitude
of books gives me a hard on.

Each writer explains my pain in many ways I can relate to;
The characters in those books reflect on the pains they deal with,
the anxiety that they eat at every meal.
The books I am reading ask me to own my pain because they are
mine – I am not a pariah.
Maybe if I write more about my love for dying, many will come and
testify about their pains and their struggles.
After all, dying does not end the pain; it begins a new circle of pain
for us and for others.

THE RELICS
Kimutai Kemboi Allan

A nasty lonely sojourn
On our vast and beautiful planet
Adorned with a few angelic deeds
A brief sojourn towards death
Man, we are made to believe
Is but a different kind of species
A warm contrast to the barbarism
Of the wild kingdom, but
Amongst us reside a cohort
Emissaries of the wicked realm
Unworking the rules of civility
Cloaked in stinking crimson vices
They wear jealousy as bright raiment
Beneath is the putrefaction of amorality
An evil assemblage of nefarious thoughts
The relics of a regrettable past!

OUR PRODIGY
Kimutai Kemboi Allan

My father's father
Colossus
Saw the sun before
It left its oriental bed.
My aunts
He wouldn't let any fool
Meddle with their tender parts
Men can be mutilated, women
Must not according to his gospel.
The village girls danced and left
To be married, young girls desecrated
My aunts tore into books with relish
My father's father
Three times a man, they
Never make that anymore!

INCIPIENT DOMESTICATION
Kimutai Kemboi Allan

A brute
Rude to the innards,
Indifferent
To the plight of his kin.
Segregative,
On nauseating terms
Race, sex, tribe and religion.
He's still rooted to the wild
A brutish paradise
Where murder is the rule
Feast or be feasted upon.
We stand in need
Of taming this rogue
A peril to the human race
We must bring to civilization
Man's feudal way of life!

It's A History

Catherine Awino

It is a history
In the epoch of I
Yes, it is a history
A soul of a heart;
a bleeding eye.

A gender at heart lives
A burdened soul
Cries deep from the ears
In decades it's been a domination.

It's been her against him
We plead for a soul
A he that strives so hard
Lots of responsibilities for a single soul.

One to protect, provide, lead but in return - no gratitude:
It's a soul that has pleaded for ages
A soul that lives a lifeless life
A life that needs care, love and support.

Gone are The Men
Catherine Awino

Gone are the times
The present we call time
Letting peace reside
For the men we honour.

Gone are the times
Labour resided for men
We forget yesterday's pain
Smile for today and tomorrow.

Gone are the times
Where we discriminate our men
Today is a new day
We sing praises for them.

Gone are the times
Where men are to provide
Duties are shared equally
We celebrate their endurance.

Gone are the times
Where gender is chosen
Our men are respected.
The sun shining in place of the moon.

Gone are the times
We give men a reason

A reason to live for tomorrow.
For the society needs men

A broken heart
Kudakwashe Paul Simbi

Broke
weak
sicky
Worthless
shameless
formless
shapeless
Bust-a- roo
Moneyless wonder
Penny-pincher
Stone broke
I am dubbed by them

At first all was well
Love birds we were
Until bad lucky caught me up
 Red handed I caught her
In her born-day gown
I couldn't look at her twice or thrice
Possessed she was... I think
She left me with a disease that cannot be cured by antibiotics or
injections
As the pain is still tattooed in my flesh
I am walking confused like a sheep without a shepherd

Wounds

boils
brokenhearted
cuts
All in one
If not four in one

Who will deliver me?
Who will teach me to love again?
Is it fate that is caught up with me?
I will mend my heart
in a solitary place
A place without a name
A no man's land

Mystic man
Nyasha Celeste Makombe

The African king on canvas
He stood, a man who has seen it all
Through the lenses of his soul love is born
His majestic crown such sophisticated elegance
Garment tainted with his origin
Mountains of hope filled with faith
Streams of spirituality flowing through purity
The soil tainted with mystery demands authority
It is through the fire of wisdom he gets spiritual grounding
He wore peace like a second skin

I stood closer to the portrait
Seeking clarity of the things unseen
He whispered " I am because you are ,
Umuntu ngumuntu ngabantu"
Frightened to the core I remained aghast
"I'm Bob Nameng" he whispered once more
I looked around seems like no one heard the portrait speak
I swear I'm going nuts
He gave me a faint smile accompanied by tear drops
I know not whether to scream or run
Dumbstruck my feet are glued to the ground

I want to tell my story got tired of hearing his story
I need just a second for one to open their ears so I can cough out
what burdens my Soul
For years I've toiled seeking a better life for my own
How sarcastic
 The same people I fight for have been drilling holes in our boat

Their burdens they cast on me
I wish .... I wish to find someone who will love me for me not
because of what I have to offer
These scars on my sleeves they can't see they are blinded by their
own desires
Chained by their expectations and unreasonable demands
I try to fight to stay afloat
Those I call my own gather to tie a huge rock on my neck to make
sure I drown
Like a feather I rise
I am who I am for it was foretold before I became
He whimpered whispered till there was nothing more to say
I remained dumbfounded as the portrait regained its original state
as if nothing happened
Who am I to tell such a wonder
Of a mystic man who refused to remain caged

The prayer
Nyasha Celeste Makombe

Forgive me father for I have sinned
Let me not taint you with barrenness
On this nocturnal visit
I have ambled gracefully in the garden of virgins
Antecedents I left speechless
Auger vivid as thunder
Besieged by unimaginable sin
The conglomerate too shallow for my soul
Demarcated from the village of my thoughts
My seeds rampant on the surface of the earth like wild fire
Forgive me father for I have sinned
Diverged from the righteous path
I feasted on the gullible
Their pride I mingled with the wind
I intend to marry none
My seeds they natured in their wombs
Fathered more than I can afford
The majority doesn't know my face nor the sound of my voice
Like a game of chess I'm forever after the Queen's
Forgive me father for I have sinned

The note
Nyasha Celeste Makombe

My son
Mirror not who I am
Honour not every step I take
Yap not for there is peace in silence
Be a man of your word and straddle not
Make not shrill demands but work for your own
Let not your eyes rove over the beauty of daughters of men
Secrete not more venom into this poisoned world
There is shame in shoddiness
Copy not my wanton disregard for women's dignity
Streaks of grey in my hair may not resemble wisdom
But years I wasted in darkness
The frightening vividness of my dream
Clearly I might not see another day
You will be left saddled with responsibilities
Let not my absence bother you

He tried

Nyasha Celeste Makombe

He sought
He suffered
He endured
Crucified by those he called his own
I sought the source of his greatness and found it not
Poverty has been his adversary from the beginning of time
Countlessly I saw him bite his lips to keep tears at bay
He toils from dawn till dusk
All he has are the scars on his sleeves
He is a slave in the land he was born to rule
History repeats itself once more
The last straw breaks the Camel's back
A stich in time saves nine

Books
Martin Chrispine Juwa

They are quicksand
That sinks the darkness of the mind
They are a burning flame
That lights up the eyes of the mind
They are a hidden path
A brave few find and trod on
Books are keys to the dreams sealed
They are a fertile plain of awareness
A lantern of hope
A greenery of human mysteries
A store of the wonders and discoveries of man
Books make the human mind eternal
When you listen to the heartbeat of books
It is like the laughter of a new-born
Peaceful and serene
Books scratch ignorance and make man a wonder
Books are mysteries
Man is eternal when his eyes see through books
When his heart is soaked in books
When knowledge seeps through his porous skin
When his shadow dances on pages

Men of War
Martin Chrispine Juwa

'For the flag, for the brethren, for the children unborn'!
The cries on the radio say.
Hardy boys and near-greying men report to their station
commanders
And finally 'ant' their way to war.
They leave starving homes and farms untilled,
They fill trains and buses, and band in camps;
Two years pass, they do not come back home
Their families mourn, splatter roses on empty graves
And forget they lived, their faces are seen in children's
But the unnamed war goes on apace,
We hear of it on the radio.
Men bearing arms in the slaughter of a brother -
As villages stand still like the scarecrow in a black Wilson hat
Only women are left; deluded
Of life's promises of fertility and laughter of children,
Only women are left; dehumanized and traumatized,
Their husbands and fathers slaughtered for a cause they barely
knew...

The essence of life
Martin Chrispine Juwa

What will we say to them, those rested souls
that wrought our lineage through ages past
when we ourselves park upon the shoals of death?
Will they welcome us with kind eyes and loving words?
Will they give us a chair in their shore to rest on?
They were on a mission to chisel a worthy legacy,
a world of wonder and love and trust
to give us an inheritance worthy more than gold.
They fought in the caves, in the trenches, in laboratories -
just to shape the world we live in today.
We shall fail to greet them with a smile when we meet,
for instead of manifesting the wonder of love they bled for,
we have destroyed the very sacred altar of oneness they left.
Indeed, there is seldom cause to celebrate today -
we have abandoned our roots. We have abandoned the essence of
life

Social Media Blues
Oscar Gwiriri

Thank you for in-boxing me,
Glad to inform you that
I am just another man like you.
We're both in the social group.
Sadly, the lady on my profile picture
Is my memorable late mother.
Sorry for the inconvenience, mate!

The bed
Oscar Gwiriri

Father was the last to wake up,
He rotated the pillowtop matress,
Did the bed in a well done manner.
Mother later remembered bed issues,
She rotated the pillowtop mattress.
Mattress position, back to square one.

The itch
Oscar Gwiriri

Last night I struggled with a damn itch,
Requested my wife to scratch my back stitch,
She declared that her rib area was itchy too,
Suddenly, she woke up, huffed off the bed,
Picked a pick and threw it over there,
Picked a sickle and threw it onto the pick,
Then picked a wire brush and returned to bed,
Suddenly, my itch vanished in vanquish style.

Closed door
Oscar Gwiriri

Up to death,
She didn't know
That he wore her
Her mom's face,
For the sweet job
To be done.

The Chat
Oscar Gwiriri

Hello dear! How was your day?
I have just passed through that lodge.
Every time I pass through this sacred place,
I remember that holy day with you,
Running my hands on your oiled body,
Under the shadows of sweet melodies
Of Hills Songs from your mobile phone.
How I long to meet you once again dear.
How I wish him to go for an outing again.
It's been a long time, this time I will kill you.
Remember to delete my chat, darling.

Two faced
Birungi Precious Uwineza

Real in the bush
Fake in the city
In the bush, you know everyone
In the city, even the chameleon is a crocodile
You have to keep up the facade for your own sake
It's all beauty outside, but drop dead ugliness on the inside

All smiles in the city
But gloomy in the heart
Cunning in the dark
Praised in the light
Good and evil, all on one face
Makes it hard to know
Which one you meet all the time

You would think sympathy is in their blood
Because they are the mothers of tomorrow
But their blood flows with malice
Greed covers their heart
And oh, their smile, it gives one chills
But all for what, simple world things?
And because one has multiple faces

It's hard for a man to take a woman home nowadays
If they do, it's just a one night stand
If it goes further, it's just an open relationship
Whereby the lady is free to cheat but not the man

And when money is scarce, she elopes with someone else
Are these the wives of tomorrow,
The mothers of the future generation
The ones whose faces changes in the presence of money
Their life is controlled by a man made things
And at the end of it all,
It's all left behind when six feet under
The despise, the whispers, the rude comments towards the men
Who lack the money or physique
At this point, you rather have money and lack physique

Safe space
Birungi Precious Uwineza

When he feels like it's all shut
And hope has faded
Anger filling his heart
Hatred running through his veins
The tears, crystal clear in his eyes
A miracle happens
Blooming his night like a flower
The anger and hatred dissipate
Because of the souls he calls home
Home to him, is not a house
Home to him, is his family

And as the night goes on,
Seeing his family with cheerful smiles
And encouraging words from his wife
He forgets about the rough day he had
And only hopes to have a better one tomorrow
So that he can make his family happy
Just like always
So that he can come home to see those brilliant smiles
Day after day, year after year.
Because home, is his safe place
Where he is allowed to break or express his feelings
Without fear of judgement.

I am the man
Birungi Precious Uwineza

Nothing is as tempting as something forbidden
Something that is already taken
But that's the point of war
We fight, to get what isn't ours
We do everything just to get what we want
And who gets hurt along the process?
That's none of our business.

Why would an eagle take a young chick?
As young as four days or even a week
Still that's none of our business
Because when that urge comes, few control it
Otherwise, it takes over and we become selfish
Likewise to the eagle, when the urge takes over,
All it thinks of is the food, not in the little bit concerned
Of the aftermath

Whether it's anger or sexual desire
The only thought running in his head
Is to get it out regardless of the consequences
After all, who will blame him
He's the man, the figurehead
And all power lies in his hands
You tattle, then say goodbye to that good life of yours
After all, whose words can be heard if it's not the men's

An act so wrong, defying the laws
But money has corrupted everything

And with it present, the line between good and evil is thin
Whether in need or not
Supporting a sin, is committing it, in a way
Superiority doesn't mean you have to violate anyone
But then, no one is brave enough to call it out
And profess it's wrongs or even sue the violators
Victims are out there
Suffering from mental health and depression
But no one hears it all,
Because it's the man, he's always right.

Persistent struggle
Birungi Precious Uwineza

He doesn't expect their kindness
Or their love for that matter
So he sucks up every insult from his bosses
Because everyone thinks he is strong
But just like every human,
He breaks but stands up again
For without challenges, there's no success
And despite what his bosses say
Discouraging him or expressing discontent
He struggles harder, so that, he can make someone happy
Be it his child, the mother or even the family

And even when he tries hard to achieve his goal,
And his mind and body can't cooperate anymore
He persists because he cannot let down all the people
Who encourage him and even look up to him
So even when he reaches his breaking point,
He strives harder and harder
Because the body cannot control him
And when he achieves his goals,
He smiles because it wasn't easy
But he also doesn't slack, because he has to maintain his success
And as long as he can give bread to his family,
Then all hope is not lost.

THE HUMAN MALE
Mutiu Odetunde

The human male
is a journeyer -- an
ethereal camel that treks
on the dunes of fate and time.
He is, in earnest, an event
of strives and existence.

The human male is a
living diary -- he reads
himself into survival.
His life is like a long
or short writing that
terminates at a full stop.

GLASSES
Mutiu Odetunde

There lives a treasure — a molded one
Kilned, painted and divinely done
To rival the finest of hollowed bisques
In terms of beauty and crushing risks

I know a fragile vase of bottled emotions
Rising and swirling in the waters of life's oceans
With motifs and reflections like a mirror art
A highly delicate piece not to be pelted at

Man is that clayware not wanting to be stoned
With words and utterances so badly intoned
An artsy piece of ceramic glare
Man is an object to handle with care.

MAN IS SPIRIT
Mutiu Odetunde

Man is a spirit,
But many don't see it;
Man's lens limit
Is top-range secret.

A soul so infinite
With grits and digits;
Man's every minute
Is aimed at winning [it].

Man is pulpit —
A sermon to revisit;
Of words quite discreet
Yet the wise discern it.

LIFE IS FICTION
Mutiu Odetunde

Life is fiction,
Our world is wholly fixed:
Fortune or fall;
Friends and foes,
Each page we read is
A flip of scenic twists.

Life is fiction,
Its script is fully themed:
Famine and food;
Fun and feud,
All make our acts
A reel of filmic deeds.

Fates fix the future,
Men tackle fixtures,
All relish fortunes but
Flukes may win the game.
Life turns a climax
And readers read in awe.

The Grip of Debt
Mathews Mhango

A mountain of bills, a daunting climb.
Too thick is this forest debt.
Tangled woods, bills like grasping thorny
vines I could never escape their grip.
That at times it scares my cracked,
holed wallet. My hungry bank
account looks malnourished as well.
Too ashamed and in tatters to save me.
A single lonely digit makes me cry.
Now chocked by debt that makes
my future hostage.
My masculinity is all but useless,
It fails to save me drowning
in this tempestuous sea of debts.
As the debt's churning waves drags me
away from the shores of debt freedom.
My manly miserable misfortunate self looks lost.
No escape from this endless din.
Loan shacks hover over me,
stalking vultures ready to pounce.
For the deal that I made with the devil himself.
But when the storm clouds of debt will clear
To the tranquil shores of freedom, I shall steer.
Though the heavy weight of debt still pains
My strength lies in resilience to reclaim my power.
As hope flickers in a distant like a star.

A Heart Forged in Iron
Mathews Mhango

His smile mystery as a ghost, lost in forgotten years
Heart is all stone cold, for the heavy weight he bears
The house, once filled with laughter, now silent as tomb
Echoes of silence impregnate the once pristine room

Children enveloped in fear, can't witness a smile in his eyes
A house too fragile, not anymore, a paradise
The wife, a wilting rose, her spirit is frail
The iron in his soul pierces her she can't exhale

Melting the iron, setting the soul alight
His soul dwells in a burnt world, nothing is right
Offers no love and care, kindness lost in a crash
The iron in his soul, burns like forge, happiness evaporates in flash.

No happiness in the crumbled home, now a fragile shell
Laughter keeps fading, loneliness and despair dwells
The iron in his soul, a heavy anchor chain him down
With every step he takes, he wears a sorrowful frown.

Chasing destiny: A marathon of flaws

Mathews Mhango

He is running this race
A marathon is what he running.
Running away
from his flaws. But they keep
on dragging him.
The flaws stuck to his heels,
Sweat stinging his dust covered eyes
Lungs burning the choked air
He is running this
race to his destiny.
His destiny keeps on
running away
from him. This race
He is running has too many
Stumbling blocks
in its race tracks, clattering like
Broken stones. they keep on
Distract him while he runs.
He sees some
Goodies that melt
in an instant. Making him forget
Where he is running to.
Heavy storm dust from
Behind stretches
Ahead of his race track
The finish line
Though in a short distance
Is obscured by the dust

From his race track.

RUGGED ROAD AND SMOOTH HIGHWAY
Mathews Mhango

Rugged road and the smooth highway,
Two paths that life can lay.
As we walk on the rugged rough road, with bumps and dips,
Others, enjoy the straight and wide highway with grip.

The rugged road in the jungle is hard to bear,
Filled with trails, tribulations, pain and care.
But those who brave its twist and turns,
Often find that wisdom burns.

For life is not a bed of roses,
And those less travelled often closes.
But those who walk its winding way,
Find strength and courage every day.

The smooth highway, on the other hand,
Is easy and comfortable, like a soft, warm band.
It lacks the challenge of the rough path,
And often leads to complacency and a lack of growth.

So, choose your path with care, my friend,
For the road you take, it my never bend.
Will you take the easy way, or will you strive,
To conquer the rugged road, and make it alive?

For in the end, it's not the road we take,

But how we handle each bump and each shake,
That shapes our character and soul,
And helps us reach our ultimate goal.

So don't be afraid to the road ahead,
Whether its rugged or smooth, don't let it daunt your head.
Embrace the journey, with courage and grace,
And you'll find your way to a brighter place.

Subjugated struggle.
Bunguswa Brian

We'd once burnt our butts,
in a quest to relieve a life sanctified
but on blisters we sat uncomfortably long,
nursing injuries of a turn so wrong-
those were wages of men's dignity deferred,
torn and drizzling in inconsistent spurts.

And we thought we had nothing to fear,
our hearts and mind were numb from the pain,
but we're now afraid of the fear that shreds us to pieces:
this fear that never ceases,
we're afraid our efforts might never gain,
life's golden prize that we held dear.

We've been dragged in anguish with no place to hide,
like an ambushed and homeless mouse;
we know the futility resident in our running-
for with renewed vigor we ended up crying,
beckoning tears that fall behind the bravery of our eyes,
reminiscent of the struggle that is oft° subjugated.

Tears under the sea.
Bunguswa Brian

Deep tears under the sea;
burns but no one can see,
nor feel or touch the soaked face.

Tears under the sea are a hemorrhage-
that breaks men with character and image,
and smolders them to the bone;
flesh without and thin.

Tears under the sea blinds the mind;
binds the soul to a devil of its kind,
interring hope when the day's fecund.

Tears under the sea conceal fears,
of life's ambers that are fierce-
brooding tragedy within,
that knows no master or king.

Men will shed tears under the mid-day sun,
blurring but mild like the moon,
that shines for their star to thrive.

Men's tears.
Bunguswa Brian

I've seen them cry,
wail and pry-
but where do their tears go,
for the happiness they forego?
Behind sullen eyes manifests grief-
of hearts laden with sadness not so brief.
And the cry emerges again,
surging with bitterness and pain.

Where do men's tears fall?
Behind hilltops like mock rainfall?
Or behind their eyes,
like melted ice?
I search my mind,
to understand a mystery of its kind;
men's tears
a manifestation of great fears.

They oft° will cry,
to soften hearts cold and dry;
of the tender feelings-
oft° absent in life's happenings.
To oblivion they've been consigned,
pitied by those never concerned.

Men wail in silent lamentation;
with hearts engulfed in deformation,
and the repercussions are tragic-

if embers of love were once intrinsic.

BURY ME.
Abdullatif Khalid

Bury me!
Deep underneath the ground,
As shadows dance and silence thuds.
Why are my rights hunted
like a thought?
My dignity unaddressed
I left like a haunted house, to fade...

Grant me not the fleeting stare
Of hollow words and empty tribute.
But bury me where freedoms burn with life
Where dignity can never perish,
a perpetual fire of liberty...

What is a man without his due?
Whose rights and voice are upheld in view?
In this demise of fleeting pants,
I'm weighed down with chains of death!
Where's my end, is it sainted or villained?

Bury me where justice buds
And doesn't stop at that but fruitions too
In sacred soil as darkness looms,
Let me rest where I will find light
My rights as a man shall be known.

A WORLD OF FEATS.
Abdullatif Khalid

Expectations weigh heavily!
I navigate the web unsteadily,
Bound by old norms but striving for a new feat,
I juggle in suits and ties so tight,
Amidst churn, emotions are hidden from sight.

The pressure;
To provide,
To succeed,
To excel,
It's a silent battle waged rarely told.

I carry burdens unseen by many eyes,
Struggling to break free from society's ties,
Forced into molds, I often suffocate,
Longing to rewrite the script to reinstate it.

In the pursuit of love,
I stumble and fall,
Afraid to show my weakness,
I lie a heart that beats,
Longing for acceptance in a world of feats.

THE CHAINS.
Abdullatif Khalid

Chaos crafts opportunity!
Within the clamor of hurried streets,
A man strides with weary feet,
Bound to the whims of a fickle fate,
In the clutch of an economy's weight.
Look
at how the markets rise and fall,
Casting shadows upon the lofty,
With decaying and withering hope.

He is in chains!
The wheels of commerce turn and spin,
A complex system, a game to win,
The hard work,
The sweat,
The need for financial stability,
The need to provide,
The bills,
Man can't rest from the hunt!

THE MUTTER OF WINGED BEINGS
Okolo Chinua

Like a syrup of glowing suns I arrive this tale a millipede with razors
for legs,
By the corner lies a broom duty-filled and exhausted...
From my son are questions...'what happens to prayers that go
unanswered?',
it sits in my throat like a lump refusing to diffuse...
My wife's eyes house hopes seeking shelter to sit...
but there are no rooms for more in these palms outstretched...
Birds,
We become those prayers winged beings mutter in flight...

THE LAUGHTER OF OPENED HOPES
Okolo Chinua

The angels throw a spear and we become rain...
I rush forward for every hollow I find..
"What cannot be filled needs remain in motion.."
Beneath the earth comes laughter and people are swallowed,
It laughs still.. What doesn't bring rain must draw lines...

In another solace is a scientist coated and dripping...
'Today I find the answers' and once more peeps, a never-ending look
into the gallows the air holds...
The house ahead comes alive as hopes continue, ants in flight...
Beneath, the laughter returns...

THE TRANSPARENCE OF THE NIGHT
Okolo Chinua

You find the scar when the night arrives,
As you nurse you whisper of how things are found better without sight...
With every peel you open, an umbrella unhinged of hooks,
First, you're the bean, wide-eyed and sharing all of you to all of them...
Next you become rice, lean and pale,
Sometimes you're the vegetable, full of life yet easily blown away.
With the last you become red, leaking out grit, fervour, virtue...
Someday you will become what you see when you sleep, a walking canvas transparent in shields...
You open these eyes as the day returns, hard and fierce...

We live Fast
David Chasumba

The six robbers partying
In a Harare night club.

We scored big. We
Top League. We

Rob class. We
Knob lass. We

Love skunk. We
Love punk. We

Live fast. We
Bite dust.

NB: This poem was inspired by Gwendolyn Brook's poem, We Real Cool.

What I really want
David Chasumba

What I really want
Is a long love letter
With love emojis
A long love letter
To lift my heart like a feather
Warm me like a hot cup of tea

What I really want
Is a long love letter
From you, my dear
Pledging that you're still near
That you still love me like a pear
That I still have a place
A space in your heart
A long love letter saying how
Much you miss me now
Saying how much you think
Of me night and day
And thirst for me like a summer drink

What I really want
Is a long love letter
Reassuring me clearly
That I am still your man
That you are still my woman
That you still love me dearly
That you're still faithful
And not knocking boots and stray

With another dude when the cat is away

What I really want
Is a long love letter
With love emojis
To cheer me here
Inside my cold cell
A long love letter, girl,
To wipe away my prison blues

Man-to-Man
David Chasumba

Man, don't share your dreams
Nor sing your secret hymns
Your brothers will plot evil schemes

Don't sell out your brothers. Don't do it
Your brothers will dump you in a water pit
And sell you off like cheap meat

Don't be easily seduced or misled
By a loose woman into her husband's bed
Man, run away from the noose instead

Man, be careful who you befriend in jail
Fake friends forget you languishing in cell
Fake friends forget you languishing in hell

Sometimes fate gives you a fit
Sometimes fate throws you down the pit
But climb your way out, bit by bit

Through life's trials, maintain strong faith
Fight the good fight, face the fate
Fight for what's right, and forgive, don't hate

Through the eyes of a child
Lucas Zulu

The aroma of dark roasted coffee
floats through the passage while the kitchen table
hums with breakfast delights. A bowl of muesli
drop from my hands and smashes to pieces
on the porcelain floor, struggling to concentrate.
Feeling blue, I withdraw into my tiny bedroom
to spill my feelings on the leaf that mum abandoned
us, just when I ache for her tender loving care,
she vanished with the helmsman, they sailed
to St Helen Island and cracked a close bond
    between us. Dad sealed it with his sense
of stability. I don't want to say we are so blessed
to have an anchor like him. Grey winter
an early bird with a blast of arctic air, frozen
to death, he wraps up all of us in fleece's and scarves.
Warm enough to smile again, as much as we don't see
our distant mum often, at least Daddy is here. His soothing
words are balm to us, the thorn of our mother's absence gone,
quelled by our father's presence. He's a tallest crane
lifting us up, above the sky-scraping task.
An Elcamino Chevrolet, all of his chubby children
hitched to its tow bar, pulling them together
    like a father into mother's shoes…

UNBROKEN

Adut Loi Akok

I do their don't
Like crowning my faith
The ring of his godship
And let it guide my tiptoes
Upon the rising waters
As I save million sinking ship
Of gods that have failed.
Men like me are captains.

I know my story is a tale of lament
In heaven for the people that have gone
before me, before I learnt the spelling
of dreams and faith and how shark baits
drive themselves onto the beach unbroken.

My mother abandoned
me between the wilderness of dreams
And rivers of dark coloured waters.

And
Guess why I still keep her words secret
Like seed corns from my text collectors?
My mother promised to sweep
the Shadows of night away from my days.
She dared herself to birth me one more
Sun that would rise from the dead
On the western horizon when the old one set.
My mother's words are the remaining seeds
I shall sow when it rains in May on this beach.

Acto de desaparición
Adelmar Ramírez

Paso los días cumpliéndole caprichos a un corazón de confituras
que desea adelantarse al envasado.
Heme aquí, recipiente maltrecho, deviniendo conserva.
Era preciso aprender
el arte de coincidir en una caja y ahuecar la voluntad
de cuando en cuando,
a diferencia
de la paloma ensortijada
entre los resortes de un truco longevo.

Hospital de juguetes
Adelmar Ramírez

falta documentar aquel sitio conventual
para juguetes rotos donde la madera mágicamente se hincha
entre los brazos del superhéroe. Así obra la pericia: ir incautando
miembros
y a la noche, abierta la cómoda,
dejar que las piezas faltantes hagan lo suyo.
Es tan frágil la naturaleza
del juego; tan necesario colmar de alas lo terrestre:
el mutante vuelve a casa, a la expansión
confinada de lo normal,
donde las pistolas engentan.
Es un caballero cambiando de oficio
tras perder su yelmo. El antídoto está ahí,
en la reparación del tullido
que amanece en un compartimiento suyo siendo otro,
con un escudo
perteneciente a su casa, sin él. Mutatis mutandis,
todo está ahí, en las refacciones

TODO HOMBRE NECESITA DEL AMOR Y DEL RELÁMPAGO

Luis Ignacio Cárdenas

(Conversación en unas de las mesas en Palmarejo)

De aquí no se levanta nadie
sin antes encontrar el nombre más adecuado que se le puede atribuir
al amanecer
y ya eso es mejor que cualquier otra promesa
no es semejante barbaridad decir que un joven enamorado o
desempleado
puede llegar a cometer actos terribles
Estimados viejos poeta de grandes hazañas y jóvenes poetas
aburridos melancólicos
permítanme hablarles un poco de mis antepasados
<< Mis manos un mapa cartográfico de pesadillas públicas >>
Está ronda de cerveza vale más que mi voz alterada cargada de
nostalgia
y muchísimas gracias
pero estoy en todo mi derecho en decir lo que me dé la gana
aunque sean ideas muy viejas
LOS ENAMORADOS NO TIENEN NADA QUE PERDER
y es el crimen otra manera de nombrar la necesidad
pero ustedes saben
el miedo produce visiones
Eso que se escucha de fondo es el brindis del bipartidismo del siglo
XXI
y ustedes bien saben que es costumbre de la gente en este país
pensar que los militares en cualquier momento
van a dar un golpe de estado
Fíjense cuántos monstruos puede engendrar la razón
y les parecerá un chiste pero el sábado pasado me dijeron

que eso de la poesía es para pobres diablos
y yo que tengo dos o tres respuestas para todo
no dije nada
y se me vino a la cabeza la canción esa
de un delincuente que busca su fortuna por una calle donde no pasa
nadie
y enseguida me dio por escribir esto
y mañana seguro escribo un manual para asaltantes de caminos
SEÑORES USTEDES ME CONOCEN
<< bueno está bien – nadie conoce mi verdadero oficio >>
soy exagerado y honesto lo más que puedo
mentir tiene su ciencia
Un hombre con los ojos cerrados
es una ruina de hombres y se tropieza con otra cicatriz y lo acobarda
el frio
sin notarlo
va construyendo su relación con las leyes de la belleza
aún en la más hostil desesperación
toda evidencia lo aturde
DAMAS Y CABALLEROS INGENUOS FANÁTICOS Y
BARBAROS
hasta ahora es que caigo en cuenta y con esto no exagero
mi conspiración es por hacer despegar el sol
en la más larga noche de tormenta y horror
hacía un lugar donde no son inútiles la verdad
ni la ternura.

Siembra
Nelson Roque Pereira

"Yo digo: no piensen en la cosecha,
sino sólo en la siembra justa".

T. S. Eliot

Entre mi cerca y la tuya
un mismo poste, el mismo alambre
que corre hasta el final
alternando las piedras
con las imprecisiones verbales,
que deshacen el infinito
en la sombra del bienvestido.
Aún quedan en la lejanía
pequeños portillos
por donde se nos van los hilos,
y rota la muralla nos hurtan
los frutos de la cosecha.

Ahora queda justo el tiempo
para demorar la siega y volver
por causas e intención
a dividir los granos
entre los dedos,
llegarán las lluvias de agosto
a subir el nivel del pozo,
a presagiar el cundiamor
y los pájaros sobre la cerca.

111

Si el destino es clavar al poste
siete grampas y un cascarón
donde crecer la orquídea,
te regalo las tempestades,
no son peores desde el horizonte
con sus cerros de humo,
basta con otear las ruinas
para saber que aún tienes casa
sólo para una siembra justa.

Torre para servir
Nelson Roque Pereira

"…como sirve al tesoro su alcancía".
Vicente Gallego

En fin y al cabo
el cuerpo es torre mar adentro
del vivir cercano.
lo que se hereda y aprende
en la estrofa de los hombres
y salta como un pez en arcos
a las ventanas de la humanidad.

Dentro de las palabras
que cortejan la mente
y el hambre de la calle
en el fango de la memoria
es una luz   un latido   el valor
por aprender a domesticar
en un sorbo las palabras "lo siento".

Después de tantos días
de sabor a ladrillo en los labios
se bordan los renglones
con los planos de la palabra
y se ancla un cuerpo más
a los límites de la vergüenza.

Torre que en fin y al cabo
concurre al rumor de las olas

113

y va al afluente que da a los ríos
a vivir lo excitante de la orilla
a sabiendas que hay aguas
que lo perdonan todo
antes de enlazar los dedos
a las manos de otro cuerpo.

Poemas de la vida de mi padre
José Carlos Monroy Rodríguez

«Y ahora solamente un poco, vuelvo tu noble aliento,
tu digna palabra, con trastabilleos, con pegoste,
con terrones, con tepalcatazos,
con palabra infantil, con palabra dicha por niños.
Que fue dicha fuera de tiempo, a despropósito.
¡Anímese, mi padre santo!»
La respuesta de un hijo a su padre. Discurso antiguo.

I

Usted me enseñó todo lo bueno, todo lo correcto [hermoso], todo lo verdadero que hay aquí sobre la tierra.
Me enseñó cómo hablar a los demás, cómo respetar a la gente, cómo obrar correctamente.
Me enseñó a ser hombre de bien [hombre de labor], a no embriagarme, a no ser de boca puerca [grosero], a no ser doble cara.
Pero no me enseñó, no me dijo todo lo que sabe.
No me dijo que la madre soltera que visitábamos habría de conocer la piel suya, la de usted.
Me dijo que era mi madrina y que a mamá no le caía.
No me dijo que su hijo en realidad era mi medio hermano.
Me dijo que era hijo de mi padrino y que él había muerto hace mucho.
No me dijo que esa mujer sola era la única.
Conocía usted a muchas más mujeres solas.
Me dijo que todas ellas eran mis madrinas.
Pero no se necesitan tantas madrinas juntas…
Me dijo que todo lo que me dijese no lo contara a mamá o a cualquier otro.

Me dijo de lo malo que es que yo mintiese.

II

Hay hombres que no deberían tener descendencia alguna.
En la pobreza y en la hambruna es donde vivirán esas criaturas.
Entre los sordos, entre los mudos es donde vivirán esas criaturas.
Hay hombres que no deberían tener descendencia alguna...
¡¡Aunque con esto esté diciendo que no debí nacer yo!!

III

Niñito nuestro, ¿Qué es lo que ha hecho?
Dijo usted que nos respetaría y no lo ha cumplido.
Niñito nuestro, ¿Qué es lo que ha hecho?
Su padre, nuestro abuelito muy cruel que era y usted vino a tomar crudelísimas maneras.
Niñito nuestro, ¿Qué es lo que ha hecho?
Sus niños, los de dentro y fuera de usted, se lo preguntamos a su persona.

A LAS DOS DE LA MAÑANA
Natalia Gómez

un hombre espera
que cambie el semáforo para cruzar

Al extremo
una mujer se sostiene
reclinada en alguna pared de la avenida

El semáforo está en rojo

Un coche se acerca
tres sujetos bajan armados
bruscos la levantan
y avientan al auto.

El semáforo sigue en rojo.

El hombre que espera,
no sabe que ella desconoce
que su cuerpo será arrojado
en una bolsa negra
rumbo a otra ciudad.

La luz ya es verde.

El agente Armani
Chaco de la Pitoreta

El individuo vestido de pantalones jens, botas de piel de lagarto y una faja café, en cuya chapa las iniciales Lr destellan como el oro mismo, encaminó sus pasos al fondo del glamuroso hotel. Enormes cortinas de cálidos colores descolgaban de las altas paredes y unos sujetos, como sacados de película, se posicionaron en diferentes puntos del lugar con más armas sobre el cuerpo que ropa misma. El guardia indicó que no se podía ingresar armas y en respuesta una fulminante mirada le dejó claro lo que tenía que hacer. En el fondo un traje oscuro de Armani cubría la lánguida fisonomía del contacto que, sentado en un mesón de seis piezas, esperaba sin prisa alguna mientras a sorbos lentos saboreaba un café.

—¿Por qué quiere hacer todo esto — expresó en español arrebatado el sujeto en el traje Armani y, acto seguido, se llevó la taza de café de nuevo a la boca, sin desviar la vista? Lr levantó la mirada, escudriñó el lugar, miró las mesas perfectamente servidas, unos comensales en el otro extremo y a las y los meceros de allá para acá poniendo y quitando cosas.
—Pues por qué el dinero que tengo no me ajusta para poder venir, como usted, a sentarme a un lugar como este, comer como usted entre gente como esta y dormir como usted sin miedo a que o para que lo despierten. Además, mis nuevos enemigos están con las Fuerzas Armadas, tienen diputados en el Congreso Nacional y en pocos días el número uno entre ellos será el presidente de Honduras, no hay forma de ganar de esta nueva etapa y no quiero terminar como mis antecesores, algunos de los cuales yo mismo aparte de la ruta pues no toleró la traición.
—Es lo que usted hará ahora con lo que nos esta proponiendo—

118

No, no es lo mismo. Ellos me traicionaron primero, yo confié en que seguiríamos haciendo negocios, les puse a disposición mi dinero y armas y ahora resulta, enterado por boca de uno de los suyos, que me quieren eliminar del camino, no extraditarme, quieren quitarme del camino. Yo siempre pierdo, pero en estas condiciones pierdo menos y, lo que es mejor ustedes tendrán a quienes quieren.

—De acuerdo. Fabricaremos pruebas, elaboraremos perfiles y quitaremos piedras del camino con su ayuda. Pero mi gobierno tiene intereses particulares más grandes para los cuales usted tiene tareas necesarias y cuyo incumplimiento dan por roto este pacto. Mi país tiene interés en ciertos gobiernos del sur, países en los que usted seguirá estableciendo vínculos comerciales que después podremos usar como prueba para justificar acciones más letales. Usted se asegurará de ponerlos en estas redes o darnos datos que nos permitan hacer perfiles (que importa si falsos positivos o no) con los cuales después podamos sacudirlos. A partir de ahora y mientras haga lo que le pidamos usted para nosotros no es un delincuente, es testigo protegido, pero para efectividad de su trabajo seguirá manteniendo este perfil y el lagarto en su laguna, y mientras todo sea como plaeamos nosotros seguiremos enarbolando la bandera de la democracia, la lucha contra el crimen organizado, narcotráfico y en el peor de los casos terrorismo en América Latina. Como prometí usted puede irse de acá cuando quiera, mi embajada le garantiza su regreso seguro y la información correcta para cada movimiento en el que sea requerido, o sus "negocios precisen".

***

El país que habito es el corazón de América, en el centro de la delgada línea que une los dos grandes pedazos de tierra que forman el continente: nos dicen centroamericanos. Se llama Honduras. Se erige en la historia con la nada gratificante memoria de ser uno de los primeros países por donde la colonización española impuso su yugo en América mediante la religión y la espada. Las memorias de traición y violencia se cuentan por todos lados y en todo tiempo, pero, a pesar de eso, sobreviven con dignidad y estoicismo pueblos originarios a los que la práctica de la barbarie y el odio a sus tradiciones y cosmovisiones no ha podido arrancar de sus suelos ancestrales. A pesar de ello, cada vez son menos y están peor.

En los últimos ciento cuarenta años Honduras es de los países del planeta en donde la línea de decrecimiento jamás ha podido invertir su proceso. Se lo debemos a 530 años de colonialismo salvaje, extirpación del gen rebelde de nuestros ancestros y ancestras y desde luego a una condena interminable de experimentos ideológicos cuyo principio y fundamento se define en el estomago, bien para someternos por hambre o para enseñarnos a que todo cuanto tocamos o poseemos lo podemos hacer mierda. Pero sin duda somos un pueblo que resiste con estoicismo incuestionable. Durante el siglo XIX fueron las empresas bananeras (chiquita, tela y estándar fruit company) quienes pusieron y quitaron presidentes a su antojo. Definieron los términos de la justicia y marcaron la ruta del expansionismo comercial. Bajo su imposición aprendimos que las tierras fértiles de Honduras sirven para alimentar a las familias que manejan el poder del mundo y que los pobres, cuando podamos, tenemos que conformarnos con la pirracha (fruta de baja calidad no es exportable) y los desechos tóxicos como el Nemagón, entre otros químicos, que se utilizaron para conseguir esa fruta.

Y ya para cuando pensábamos que el tiempo, el implacable, el que siempre pasa nos liberaría de ese intervencionismo se vienen las fuerzas armadas, su escuela de las Américas, sus escuadrones de la muerte y el narcotráfico. En los recientes cuarenta años hemos ido cada cuatro, como idiotas, a las urnas para ejercer un sufragio que no llegó ha ser ni el remedo de las peores expresiones de democracia y, contrario a todo, fue estableciendo unas formas de gobierno más definidas y enmarcadas en la corrupción y la impunidad que las mismas dictaduras que alguna vez, con las armas, en nuestros pueblos combatimos. Los narcotraficantes, criminales comunes, natos, se dieron cuenta de la fragilidad de la democracia, lo inmoral de sus administradores y aprovecharon la coyuntura.

Es esta historia endeble y plagada de infortunios y la posición geográfica la que vuelve a Honduras un disco indispensable en la gran columna vertebral del narcotráfico continental y un punto estratégico para la geopolítica. De cualquier parte del cono sur donde se produzcan drogas, cuyo destino sean los mercados norteamericanos, ineludiblemente tienen que pasar por este territorio y, en viceversa y para nuestra desgracia, cualquier estrategia neocolonizadora, que el gobierno con la bandera de las cincuenta estrellas quiera imponer en la región, marcha desde las bases militares que sirven de oficina a la Central de Interferencia anglosajona, por sus siglas conocida como CIA.

Por eso los ataques a dirigentes de discurso diferenciado en toda Latinoamérica fueron fácilmente justificados desde la vinculación con las drogas usando, desde luego, la capacidad de organizar y la libertad de operar con la que Lr, ahora agente del crimen encubierto, preparaba los perfiles y fabricaba las pruebas. Pero no todo llegaba hasta ahí, en los días siguientes y solo después del ensayo perfecto hecho en Honduras, los Golpes de Estado se fueron reproduciendo sistemáticamente en todos aquellos gobiernos cuyo discurso les hacía parecer diferente a los intereses del capitalismo expuesto. Y la violación de la soberanía de los pueblos esta vez, y como alguna vez lo hicieron lo hiciera los Estados Unidos en estos territorios, llegó con sujetos de rostro tierno, abrazo afable y misericordia divina. Los

121

mismos marines solo que en ves de un rifle cargando la biblia y en ves de secuestrar gobernantes secuestrando sistemas y consolidando sus dictocracias.

Lr primero se hizo amigo de políticos locales, apoyó sus campañas y les financió proyectos de desarrollo, al mismo tiempo les invitó a sus haciendas, les dio ganado, buenos regalos de cortesía y luego les compartió un poco de su ganancia. Después se fue al segundo nivel con los diputados, estos lo conectaron con los operadores de justicia principalmente militares, policías y jueces de los tribunales, hasta que finalmente entró a la escena electoral y hoy, como una nueva franquicia comercial, define como debe ser y quien el presidente Honduras. Y esto es Honduras.

***

Con fluidez natural el dinero de Lr empezó a circular por todo el país a vista y paciencia de quienes debieron, de ser real la ley, hacer algo para detenerlo. El Don antes de su nombre se fue haciendo común, aunque para entonces apenas llegará a los cuarenta y su apariencia, al menos en la forma de vestir, no superara la de un muchacho de esos que van en los pikup ford último modelo con las canciones de banda y narcorridos a todo volumen.

En las iglesias fueron apareciendo santos con leyendas de agradecimiento marcadas con su nombre. Prédicas y homilías le fueron dedicadas por entero a su bondad y amor al próximo, al tiempo que curas y pastores le guardaban una butaca los domingos en la fiel esperanza de un jugoso diezmo o limosna al final del ritual religioso. La feligresía vio crecer sus templos y la fe en la justicia, el amor al prójimo, la solidaridad entre los pobres pasó a segundo plano. El mecías anunciado tantas veces había llegado y construía grandes complejos habitacionales y a cambio solo pedía que le dejaran tener una cacita en el centro de todas para cuando fuera a visitarles, curaba enfermos o los mandaba al médico que en estos casos es lo mismo, liberaba presos y condenaba a los traidores. De esto último nadie hablaba, aunque todos lo sabían.

Iba a las escuelas y las mejoraba, pero en las comunidades donde no las había levantaba nuevas. Arreglaba los caminos, donaba para los proyectos de solidaridad social y no faltaba con su caballo pura sangre en los desfiles de la feria del pueblo. Se hizo normal encontrarle en los restaurantes y en el mejor de los casos pedir que atendieran a todos los clientes en lo que quisieran, pero de la factura se hacía responsable. En días complicados cerraba todo, sacaba a la gente y se quedaba solo, ahogando penas en botellas de licor, en una esquina junto a la puerta, con la pistola en la mano, sin quitarle la vista a su hombre de confianza a sabiendas de que él, como en aquellos días, podría matarle.

Sin embargo, la promesa de ser el empresario reconocido y respetado se fue postergando. Los susurros sobre sus vínculos con el crimen organizado, sobre el origen de su dinero y la leyenda del lagarto, destino final de quienes se atrevían a cuestionarlo o traicionarlo, se fueron haciendo parte de la leyenda que forjó el mito. Intentó por todos los medios silenciar los susurros, pero le resultó imposible, a la palabra dicha cuando alza vuelo no hay como cortarle las alas o limitarle oídos. Odiado por unos, amado por otros.

***

A mi pueblo llegaron primero los rifles que los libros y los batallones que las escuelas. A los primeros jóvenes los educaron militares en

123

vez de profesores y por eso aprendieron a disparar antes que ha leer y escribir. De esa primera generación viene Lr y por eso para él la muerte no es un misterio y matar no es anormal. Nació pobre entre los pobres, pero con enormes ambiciones de poder y dinero. Fue su padre quien lo acercó al Toro — no será muy inteligente patrón, dijo su padre, pero le aseguro que esta formado para serle muy útil—. Entonces el toro, luego de una rápida revisión lo empleo por primera vez. Primero distribuía droga en el colegio entre estudiantes, después le asignaron el control del territorio y luego lo llamaron a proteger al Toro. Se volvió su mano derecha en los negocios y su sicario más efectivo tanto que, un par de años después fue la misma pistola que juró proteger al Toro la que lo mató. Entonces emergió Lr como amo y señor. Como el más grande.

Entrado en las altas esferas del negocio descubrió que ahí se movían más personas de las que pensaba y con más poder del que imaginaba. Dueños de bancos, megatiendas, transportistas, agroindustriales, ganaderos y constructoras le invitaron a invertir con ellos. Alcaldes, diputados, gobernadores y ministros le juraron amistad sincera y el apoyo necesario. Militares, policías, jueces y abogados se pusieron a sus ordenes para proteger el negocio y asegurar resultados. Lr, lo vio caer a sus pies, rendirse e idolatrarlo, su ego tocó el cielo. A cambio abrió sus caletas y lanzó migajas a los menos importantes; y con los más pesados estableció alianzas, preparó traslados, planificó asesinatos, justificó proyectos, lavó dólares que ya habían sido lavados por la Despreocúpate Estoy con Alzhéimer que por sus siglas se conoce como DEA a cambio de sus favores para hacer caer a otros.

Pero el dinero y el poder no lo es todo. Las ambiciones no tienen limites y en poco tiempo Lr vio emerger a otros con ganas de ser él o deshacerse de él. Entonces con su nueve milímetros cacha de oro y esmeraldas incrustadas, donadas directamente de una de las caletas que antaño fuera de Pablo Emilio, su ídolo, impuso sus reglas y satisfizo sus antojos, Pero no encontró el respeto deseado, siempre se sintió menos ante los empresarios con el apellido raro, los blanquitos de la capital, los que podían aparecer en cualquier espacio sin tener que fingir porque el resto de la sociedad da por hecho lo que son, como él, solo que en el otro lado, aunque ambos sean el mismo tipo de criminales. —No hay diferencia, refutaba mal humorado entre sus vacas y caballos pura sangre—. Olvidaba que algunos tenían la facultad de delinquir de manera legal, él no.

Esos desaires, saberse menos cuando seguro tenía más y la imposibilidad de sentirse seguro y legal en un futuro próximo le hicieron aceptar el reloj y los anteojos que la DEA le sugirió usar. Con esos artefactos se hicieron trasmisiones en vivo, se grabaron reuniones y se registraron pactos comerciales con rostros y personas que, desde otras ópticas, jamás se habría pensado que estuvieran ahí.

Para cuando las rencillas se volvieron inmanejables entre ellos y las dudas se fueron haciendo fuertes, Lr ya había olido su final en los perfumees caros que con su dinero compraban eso que alguna ves consideró socios. Pensó en él mismo, aquellos días atrás, cuando con la pistola que el toro le dio para protegerlo él lo extinguió de tajo junto a las dos generaciones de su familia que se podían interponer en sus ambiciones. "A mí no me harán lo mismo", se dijo.

***

El día de la toma de imposición el discurso del ilegal presidente fue una clara amenaza a los enemigos del proyecto económico y político que se instauraría. Fue como si en cada palabra recordará que aquel helicóptero no había caído en vano y aquella detención en el aeropuerto internacional no se quedaría así. Haré lo que se tenga que hacer, sentenció. Las fuerzas armadas retomaron su práctica de hacer desfiles cívicos por las ciudades del país exhibiendo su arsenal armamentista y su entreguismo absoluto a las nuevas formas de gobierno y justicia diseñadas para el país. Una interminable lista de extraditables, en los días siguientes, se iba haciendo pública, aunque no oficial, en distintas regiones del país. Masacres: ajustes de cuentas según la policía que no investiga, desaparecidos, falsos positivos expuestos de forma dantesca en vías publicas, muestras ineludibles del mensaje subliminal que el nuevo cartel del terror dejaba para sus adversarios. Bandas criminales de varias zonas del país fueron desarticuladas y exhibidas públicamente, incautaciones de drogas, propiedades muebles e inmuebles, caletas de dinero, sociedades mercantiles, más extraditables. De un momento a otro aquel territorio que estaba plagado de carteles de la droga e innumerables testaferros - lavadores de activos - se convirtió en territorio de un solo cartel y en paraíso fiscal de una pequeña elite económica experta en blanquear capital.

Había que preparar la partida.

***

En una corte de justicia internacional Lr, testigo protegido, comparece en una acusación criminal contra un narcotraficante hondureño, cuyo ego lo llevó a poner sus iniciales en los kilos de cocaína que traficaba. Su mirada es fría, como la misma muerte, y sus palabras retumban, como los mismos ecos de las pistolas, en la atribulada cabeza del narco enjuiciado. No se le nota un solo signo de arrepentimiento, al contrario, habla con tanta naturalidad como si nada temiera, como si todo el mal causado le hubiera insensibilizado el alma. Describe con parsimonia cada hecho y encuentro sostenido

126

con el sujeto vestido de naranja y grilletes en pies y manos frete a él, le clava una mirada burlesca, lo humilla como alguna ves se sintió humillado él.

Un año antes aquellos que le juraron protección le arrebataron todo. Sentado en una butaca del restaurante, franquicia internacional generalmente usada por personajes de su estilo en la capital industrial hondureña, estableció las coordenadas y definió los términos para el viaje. — No voy a permitir que me usen como publicidad bien por que me extraditen o me exterminen, ahora es cuando toda la información recabada tendrá sentido. — No podré salvarte casi nada, le dijo en tono complicado el agente Armani. Pero a Lr ya no le importaba. Se lamentó por la seguridad de los animalitos en el zoo, la comida de su lagarto y lo que pasaría con su familia en esta ausencia, pero no había nada que se pudiera hacer por ahora. — Tranquilo, le aseguró el agente Armani, tu familia va a estar bien. La mayoría vendrán con nosotros a casa, con otras identidades y todo el dinero que has conseguido en los negocios establecidos desde que sos un encubierto, otros seguirán acá, bajo perfil, infiltrándose, tratando de salvarte algunas cosas y manteniendo el control. — me basta, susurró casi derrotado. El agente Armani se despidió con un nos vemos pronto y la mano dando golpecitos en el hombro de Lr. Este se quedó quieto, no dijo nada y se limitó a observar el corte de carne estilo New York reposando en su plato. Lo cortó lento, masticó largo y lo tragó hondo… en cada acto imaginó a los que lo traicionaron y fue sintiendo la rabia que lo contenía.

Los ecos de la doble moral en la justicia internacional son un himno en Honduras. Acapara portadas, despierta la imaginación y revive la esperanza. Pero es tan cuestionable como efectiva. Se dice por ahí, que dicen por allá, que algunos criminales que inundaron de sangre y drogas este terruño andan como si nada, libres como el viento, como si el solo hecho de señalar a otros les diera derecho a vivir impunes del mal causado. Pero que se puede esperar de una justicia administrada por un país que no reconoce otra ley que no sea la suya y otra normalidad que la que desde sus intereses se impone.

Sentado en el corredor de la casa veo por la rendija del cerco y me pregunto cuando habrá otra Honduras, cuando esos parajes hermosos que se pintan solos y se llenan de atardeceres podrán amanecer a un mejor día. Es utopía. Mientras la droga sea un negocio rentable capaz de sostener economías globales y adicciones mundiales, el hambre una condición general entre mi gente y los jueces internacionales sigan requiriendo de testigos protegidos para justificar su efectividad este cuento, que hoy les cuento, será una historia de amor redactada en un país en donde la realidad supera la ficción.

Mansilla en Egipto: la distancia entre la palabra y el suceso
Felicitas Casillo

"África tiene en la eternidad su destino, donde hay hazañas, ídolos, reinos, arduos bosques y espadas. Yo he logrado un atardecer y una aldea", Jorge Luis Borges.

En *Una excursión a los indios ranqueles*, el escritor argentino Lucio V. Mansilla menciona sus viajes por el mundo, aunque no se detiene mayormente en ellos. Esos viajes, sin embargo, configuraban la mirada que el militar tuvo sobre la propia realidad argentina. Sobre su condición existencial de viajero, Mansilla sostiene:
Los médanos de la Verde estaban a la vista, y es probable que, en mi caso, otro viajero no se hubiera detenido. Pero la experiencia es madre de la ciencia, yo me reía de algunos de mis oficiales que, viendo el objetivo tan cerca, murmuraban: ¿por qué se parará aquí este hombre?
Ellos no habían recorrido como yo, cuatro partes del mundo, en buque de vela, en vapor, en ferrocarril, en carreta, a caballo, a pie, en coche, en palanquín, en elefante, en camello, en globo, en burro, en silla de manos, a lomo de mula y de hombre. (1984, p. 374-375)

A los 18 años, en 1851, Mansilla viajó al norte de África, y recién en 1863, más de 10 años más tarde, publicará *Recuerdos de Egipto*, mientras que en 1870 comenzará a escribir y publicar *Una excursión a los indios ranqueles* en el periódico *La Tribuna*. Es decir, existe casi una década entre los tres acontecimientos: el viaje hacia El Cairo, el relato de ese viaje y la excursión a los ranqueles. El viaje a Egipto apenas se menciona en *Una excursión*: "No he visto jamás en mis correrías por la India, por África, por Europa, por América, nada más solitario que estos montes del Cuero" (1984, p. 61). Luego, se lee la referencia, de tono surrealista, a unos versos de Manzoni, durante un sueño en el que Mansilla se figuraba a sí mismo como un pequeño Napoleón: "Dall'Alpi alle *Piramide* / Dal Manzanarre al Reno" (1984, p. 71). También aparece en *Una excursión* alguna ocasional metáfora, en otro sueño también descabellado, acerca de un monumento que parecía egipcio, propio de un faraón (1984, p. 173). Finalmente, alguna vaga alusión sobre la metempsicosis (1984, p. 224).

Si bien, entonces, las menciones a Egipto no son cuantiosas en *Una excursión*, sí el lector puede suponer, en cambio, que la experiencia del viaje configura notablemente la mirada del autor. Así lo confiesa el propio Mansilla en un párrafo memorable:

[D]espués de haber recorrido la Europa y la América, de haber vivido como un marqués en París y como un guaraní en el Paraguay; de haber comido mazamorra en el Río de la Plata, charquicán en Chile, ostras en Nueva York, macarroni en Nápoles, trufas en el Périgord, chipá en la Asunción, recuerdo que una de las grandes aspiraciones de tu vida era comer una tortilla de huevos de aquella ave pampeana [ñandú o choique] en Nagüel Mapo, que quiere decir "Lugar del Tigre". (1984, p. 3)

Y también en *Una excursión*:

Es menester haber pasado por ciertas cosas, haberse hallado en ciertas posiciones, para comprender con qué vigor se apoderan ciertas ideas de ciertos hombres; para comprender que una misión a los ranqueles puede llegar a ser para un hombre como yo, medianamente civilizado, un deseo tan vehemente, como puede ser para cualquier ministril una secretaría en la embajada de París. (1984, p. 8)

En *Recuerdos de Egipto*, Mansilla describe su experiencia del viaje a El Cairo. Su mirada, como él mismo apunta al comienzo, no es la del viajero maduro, sino que observa aquella tierra extraña con los

130

ojos de un joven: "No. A los diez y ocho años, no viaja el hombre como filósofo, ni como observador, ni como sabio" (1863, p. 228). Doce años después, al referirse a ese viaje, "madura" la experiencia desde la distancia temporal y enriquece los recuerdos con comentarios y apreciaciones.

La edición del texto en la que se basa la presente apostilla es la original, de 1863, en *La revista de Buenos Aires*, tomo III. La publicación era dirigida por los abogados Miguel Navarro Viola y Vicente G. Quesada, y fue impresa en la Imprenta de Mayo de la calle Moreno 341 y 343. Llamativamente, todas las palabras que llevan la letra "g" fueron, en cambio, escritas con "j": "imajen", "pájinas", "esfinjes", etcétera. Por la generalización del error, más que de una equivocación ortográfica, es posible que se trate de alguna falencia en el proceso de impresión. Estilísticamente, *Recuerdos de Egipto* está lejos de la altura de *Una excursión a los indios ranqueles*. Mansilla mismo lo reconoce en el primer párrafo como un diario "insulso e imperfecto".

Al igual que *Una excursión*, *Recuerdos* está escrito en primera persona, y aunque narra una experiencia pasada, el relato se concreta con verbos en presente. Como en el texto referido a los ranqueles, Mansilla alude excentricidades culinarias como ejemplo de la experiencia cosmopolita: "[Los viajeros] cansados del trópico van a ver salir el mezquino sol de Europa, y a pedir en las fondas de Londres y París un plato de pies de elefantes guisados, como si estuvieran en Agra, Delhi o Benarés" (1863, p. 232). La mención de platillos continúa cuando compara el sabor de la giba de los camellos con la ubre de la vaca y la dulzura de su carne con la de las yeguas (1863, p. 235). También vuelve a referirse a la alimentación de los "tourist" cuando relata cómo y qué se pide en un salón de hospedería. Aun así, Mansilla, con aire militar y una austeridad que

131

también aparecerá *en Una excursión*, afirma, no sabemos si con algo de ironía también: "No recuerdo precisamente el detalle del precio de todos los vinos, pues, en aquel entonces, lo mismo que ahora, pertenecía a la sociedad de la templanza" (1863, p. 411).

Luego, el autor se embarca —el texto sugiere otra metáfora de navegación: las tropillas de camellos son "bajeles" que surcan el desierto— en la descripción de un repertorio de personajes rudos, en su mayoría masculinos: los beduinos que cantan con tambores para animar a los camellos; los vendedores de baratijas que gritan "antiq, antiq!", y los trabajadores que construían justo en ese año el canal de Suez. En modalidad descriptiva también se refiere el autor al desierto mismo y a sus atardeceres incomparables, y en medio del relato hilvana alusiones a la propia tierra, como quien tensa un hilo que lo guiará también de regreso.

Al referirse al vellón que una vez al año pierden los camellos, compara los tejidos que traman los egipcios con los de Catamarca y los de Santiago del Estero. Luego, en un párrafo de gran belleza, Mansilla incluye construcción subjetiva semejante a la del párrafo antes citado sobre las ostras de Nueva York y la tortilla en Nagüel Mapo:

Yo he visto entrarse el sol en la gramínea y desierta Pampa; en el océano onduloso y sin límites, que predispone la mente a una sublime meditación; en las selvas espesas del camino de Calcuta a Chandernagor, en el golfo azulado, donde Nápoles baña sus plantas como orgullosa y coqueta Náyade del Mediterráneo; en los picos nacarados de los Alpes; en la cumbre del Corcovado, monstruo que se refleja en el verdoso espejo de las aguas de la bahía de Río de Janeiro; en las márgenes donde corre la linfa cristalina de los dos grandes ríos en los cuales abrevan sus ganados cuatro provincias argentinas, y en la meseta de Paraguarí, desde donde se divisa una red de riachuelos que se pierden serpenteando en la lontananza. Pero jamás he contemplado un cuadro tan grandemente melancólico y siniestro, ni cuyos tintes tenga tan presentes, como la puesta del sol en el desierto adyacente a Suez. (1863, p. 240).

La melancolía reaparece al citar unos versos del escritor coterráneo Esteban Echeverría:

No recuerdo si pensé en la patria. Pero debí pensar. ¿Quién no piensa en ella cuando está en el extranjero?
Es la hora en que los tristes corazones
ven la imagen sombría,
de la esperanza que los sustentaba,
desvanecerse con la luz del día.
Echeverría (Mansilla, 1863, p. 409)

Más avanzado el texto, en una oración donde se observa alguna incongruencia verbal: "El frío *era* intenso; *cae* un rocío copioso, parecido al de nuestra Pampa" (1863, p. 413). ¿En qué presente cae el rocío sobre el desierto de Suez? ¿Acaso cuando el joven Mansilla lo visitaba o, más bien, cuando el Mansilla maduro lo recuerda? ¿Y cuándo fue intenso ese frío? ¿En Egipto, en la Pampa o en los pensamientos de un hombre que recuerda en la patria cómo recordaba la propia tierra desde un país remoto?

Mansilla es sin dudas sugerente. Su lectura estimula las preguntas, las comparaciones, la curiosidad sobre lo propio y lo otro, lo lejano, lo extraño, lo aún no comprendido. De un modo diferente a como lo hace en *Una excursión*, en donde se refería largamente a la peculiaridad de la lengua y de la traducción, en *Recuerdos de Egipto* también alude el asunto de la figuración, esta vez, artística:

133

Pero cuando el sol va ocultándose completamente, cuando los últimos resplandores de su disco destellan apenas una especie de vapor rojizo, el cual parece extenderse sobre toda la tierra, he ahí el momento sobre todo en que el desierto es indescriptible. (…) *No; el arte copia, imita; pero no reemplaza a la naturaleza, ni aun cuando se trate de la parte gráfica que es lo más rudimentario.* (…) *María Santísima era infinitamente más hermosa que a Madonna de Rafael.* (1863, p. 408)

Mientras que, en *Una excursión*, Mansilla traduce la realidad ranquel a los lectores de la *La Tribuna*, en *Recuerdos* parece haber una voluntad, por un lado, intimista: el joven Mansilla dicta sus memorias al Mansilla maduro, que las sopesa y comenta, como un aventurero que emprende el inventario de sus hallazgos. En *Una excursión*, el escenario es la frontera, una frontera móvil, un sitio en disputa: en el fondo, el entero desierto argentino. En *Recuerdos*, el desierto de Suez es un espacio y un tiempo: un paisaje que "no es de este mundo", y un momento, en el que la belleza del desierto es "indescriptible". También es el desierto la propia memoria, la misteriosa distancia entre la palabra y el suceso.

ABSENTIA
Clemency Madyangove

The sun beat down on Kumusha Royal International Airport as Izwi stepped off the plane, his heart heavier than the backpack he carried. It had been seven years since he'd left The Kingdom of Ekhaya, seeking a better life abroad. But as he saw the familiar faces of his wife, Chichi, and his daughter, a sparkle of inspiration, he knew he'd made a mistake. The country that he remembered as desolate and dry had been transformed, filled with new life and development. Around him, Izwi saw a country that had flourished. The smell of fresh fruit and spices wafted through the air, mingling with the chatter of excited travelers. The terminal was filled with people in colorful, traditional attire, their laughter echoing off the walls. In the distance, he could see a towering skyscraper that hadn't existed when he left. It was as if he had stepped into a different world, a world he could never have imagined seven years ago. He remembered the day he'd left The Kingdom. The airport had been a sea of anxious faces, and the customs officers had been gruff and surly. It had taken hours to get through the lines, and the smell of sweat and fear had hung in the air. But today, everything was different. The passport control officer smiled as she stamped his passport, and the customs official nodded pleasantly as he waved him through.

Izwi's feet felt like lead as he made his way down the airport's bustling corridor. He could barely see through the blur of his own tears, but he knew Chichi's unmistakable silhouette even from tear smeared lenses. She was beautiful, her smile radiating like the midday sun. And his daughter, her eyes shining with a curiosity he could barely comprehend. Izwi's heart leapt into his throat as Chichi wrapped her arms around him, her embrace warm and familiar. For a moment, he was lost in the scent of her hair and the touch of her skin, and all his doubts and fears vanished. "I missed you," she

135

whispered, her lips brushing against his ear. He smiled, his eyes filling with tears. "I missed you too," he replied. "More than you could ever know."

As they pulled apart, Izwi turned to his daughter. She was shy at first, but when he knelt down to her level and held out his hand, she reached out and grabbed it, curiosity sparkling in her eyes. "Hello, little one," he said, his voice trembling with emotion. "I'm your baba." She looked up at him, her eyes a deep, familiar brown. "Baba," she repeated, and he felt his heart break open. "I'm so sorry, Tariro," Izwi said, unable to keep the regret from his voice. "I never should have left." Chichi placed a gentle hand on his shoulder. "It's okay, my love," she said. "What's important is that you're here now." He nodded, looking from Chichi to their daughter. "And I'm never leaving again," he vowed, a new sense of purpose growing within him "I'm home."

As they made their way through the crowded airport, Izwi noticed a subtle change in Chichi's demeanor. Her smile had become more forced, and she seemed distracted, glancing around as if she was worried someone might see them. "Are you okay?" he asked as they reached the car. She smiled, but it didn't quite reach her eyes. "Of course," she replied. "I'm just happy to have you back. But I think we should hurry.

Izwi felt a strange mix of pride and jealousy as he climbed into the sleek, modern SUV that Chichi drove. Back when he'd left, most people were lucky to have a car at all, let alone one that was brand new and so luxurious. The road they drove on was smooth and wide, with streetlights and newly planted trees lining either side. As they passed through the city, Izwi couldn't help but notice how much had changed.

"This is incredible," he said, trying to hide the hint of bitterness in his voice. "You must be doing well, this side" Chichi nodded, her expression guarded. "We've worked hard," she said. "And we've had help from...friends." Izwi looked at her, trying to read the meaning behind her words. "Friends?" he repeated, a sinking feeling beginning to form in his chest.

Izwi gazed out the window of the car, his family chatting and laughing around him. But their conversation, peppered with the latest street lingo and inside jokes, was like a foreign language to him. He felt adrift, a stranger in his own family, separated from them by the distance of experience. As they passed by the bustling city streets, Izwi longed for the familiar warmth of home, the sound of the village drums, and the crackle of the fire under the stars.

The house they pulled up to was a far cry from the small, one-bedroom apartment he remembered. It was a spacious, modern villa, surrounded by lush gardens and a high wall. Chichi opened the gate with a remote, and Izwi couldn't help but feel like he was a stranger in his own home. Chichi turned to him, a smile playing on her lips. "Welcome home, Izwi." But her words felt heavy with unspoken truths. "This is amazing," he said, his voice full of awe and confusion. "I don't understand. How did you afford all this? Who helped you?" Chichi gave him a long, searching look. "I did what I had to do, Izwi," she said. "I wanted a better life for our family. And while you were gone, I found a way that could help me make things happen." Izwi felt his stomach drop. "And remember you were remitting money to us!" she elaborated.

After the long journey, Chichi insisted that Izwi take a warm bath to relax. She lit scented candles and added fragrant herbs to the water, letting him immerse in silence for a while soaking into the Kingdom of Ekhaya's atmosphere. When he emerged, the smell of traditional spices greeted him, reminding him of all that he had missed. They sat down to a meal that was both familiar and foreign, savoring the flavors and each other's company. After a delicate meal Chichi lead him to the bedroom, where spacious linen awaited them. Izwi sank into the soft mattress, marveling at the luxury of the bed.

Chichi lingered in the doorway for a moment, a strange look on her face. Then she crossed to the window and drew the curtains closed. "You need to rest," she said, her voice soft and sad. "And then, we can talk." Izwi nodded, but he felt, that rest wouldn't come easy.

The sun's fingers crept across the wall, rousing Izwi from sleep. Chichi's eyes were alight with desire as she gently shook his shoulder. "Wake up, my love," she whispered, her voice as soft as the linen they shared. "It's time for us to remember." And so they did, their bodies finding each other like pieces of a puzzle they had forgotten how to complete. They moved slowly, lingering in every embrace, in every kiss, in every sigh. When the last traces of their lovemaking had faded away, they stepped into the shower together, letting the hot water wash over their skin. Chichi tilted Izwi's head back and rinsed the soap from his hair, her touch gentle and tender. "Today," she murmured, "I have a surprise for you. Something that will remind you of what we once had, and what we can have again." Izwi smiled with a sigh of relief, and a tear drop slightly hidden in the midst of the shower's spray.

A few minutes later, he blinked in confusion as he entered the dining room. There, seated at the table, was a notorious familiar face from his past—Mboko, his college mate from years ago. A nervous smile played across Mboko's lips as he rose to greet Izwi, who still stood in the doorway, trying to process this unexpected turn of events. "Please, sit," Chichi said, gesturing toward an empty seat. "Advocate Mboko has something important to discuss with us, but we can talk after breakfast." Izwi lowered himself into the chair, his back stiff and his eyes fixed on his plate. Adv. Mboko's hand trembled as he lifted a piece of fruit, his gaze darting around the room as though searching for answers. Chichi stared out the window, a portrait of her former self hung above her shoulder, a reminder of the promises they had made before life intervened. The air hung heavy with unspoken words and remembered pain. Each sip of coffee, each glance between husband and wife, spoke volumes about the shattered dreams they once shared. As the sun streamed through the windows, painting the room with golden light, Izwi's eyes settled on a family portrait above the mantelpiece. The faces of his wife and child stared back at him. it was as if time has stood still in that moment, frozen in the frame in oblivious to the turmoil that lay ahead. Finally, Adv. Mboko cleared his throat. "I think it's time we talked." Chichi's expression hardened, like the stone statues in the courtyard outside. Izwi's heart thudded in his chest, pounding a warning he'd ignored for too long. Adv.Mboko's voice was solemn as he began. "Izwi, Chichi and I...well, we've been working together while you were away. She's a remarkable woman, and we...we developed a close relationship. We've even discussed—" He paused, struggling to find the right words. "A future of further working together." Izwi confused and trying to process the words, Adv Mboko passed through to him a folder "This is your statement of your financial remittance and how they were invested." Adv. Mboko's voice gaining composure.

As Izwi's eyes scanned the numbers on the documents, his hands trembled. This was no mere accounting of past transactions, but a record of his mistakes, his absence, and his failure. Chichi had turned his omission into something tangible, something solid, and something that could outlast the fragile human heart. And yet, even in the face of his own inadequacies, he felt a strange sense of relief. The sigh that escaped his lips was not one of victory, but of surrender. Izwi realized that he had been clinging to a dream, a memory of the past that no longer existed. The woman who had once loved him had become a stranger, a force of nature he no longer knew how to navigate. And yet, a part of him still yearned for that old love, that old sense of belonging. He wondered if that love could ever be resurrected, or if it had died along with his misguided dreams of success. Chichi's gaze flitted back and forth between her husbands, a woman caught in the judgment of her own decisions. She hoped to be cheered for a job well done, for a great family reunion and, a new beginning. But the look in Izwi's eyes told her that this period was a moment of a sad story. Izwi was once again lost in a trance of his unusual demonic neglect. "You have done well," Izwi said finally, his voice heavy with sorrow. He stood from the table, pushing his chair back with a scrape that echoed in the silence. He looked at Chichi and Adv. Mboko, his eyes full of questions that he knew would never be answered. Without another word, he turned, take the car keys and left the room, his footsteps echoing down the hall as he walked away from the life he'd once known. Chichi closed her eyes, the burden bearing down on her like a weight she'd never truly shed.

Izwi got into the car and drove, the cityscape blurring into the countryside as he sped away from the life he had left behind. The road seemed to stretch on forever, a metaphor for the vast emptiness he felt inside. At some point, he pulled over at a roadside bar, seeking refuge in the amber warmth of a drink or two. As he stepped into the dimly-lit establishment, Izwi felt the weight of his journey lift ever so slightly. The air was thick with smoke and the murmurs of travelers swapping stories. He took a seat at the bar and ordered a drink, the world around him fading into a haze of alcohol and noise. As the night wore on, Izwi found himself drawn into conversations about work, politics, and love. Topics that once felt distant and impersonal now taking on a newfound weight and meaning. In the midst of this drunken haze, a thought occurred to Izwi. He was a stranger in his own form, a man lost in his fallacy. But there was one place that would always welcome him back with open arms—the village of his youth, where the dust of the roads still carried the scent of his childhood, and where the faces of his ancestors watched over him from the sacred shrine.

As the sun began to rise over the horizon, casting its light on the winding road ahead, Izwi started his car and began the long drive back to his village. The highway transformed into a dirt road, the bustling city transformed into a landscape of rolling hills and grazing livestock. He drove on, through winding roads and over bumpy terrain, until finally, he came upon a familiar sight—the old wooden gate that led to his family village.

Izwi's eyes widened as he took in the sight of his village. Gone were the thatched roofs and subsistence farming techniques of his youth. In their place were neat rows of modernized houses and commercialized farms, with tractors and irrigation systems dotting the landscape? Solar panels lined the rooftops, and schoolchildren chattered as they walked to and from class, their schoolbags bulging with books. Izwi's heart swelled with pride as he walked through his village. He had once dreamed of leaving this place behind, of making a name for himself in the city. But now, he saw that the village had been doing just fine without him. In fact, it was thriving, a testament to the hard work and ingenuity of its resilient people.

When the village elders heard that Izwi had returned, they gathered in the village square to greet him. They sang traditional songs of welcome, clapping their hands and stomping their feet in a rhythmic dance that Izwi remembered from his youth. "We knew you would come back to us," said one of the elders, his voice deep and wise. "You may have forgotten the ways of our village, but we have not forgotten you," said another elder. "You are a part of our history, a thread in the tapestry of our people. Do not despair at what has passed, but look forward to what lies ahead." Izwi nodded, a sense of peace settling over him. As the weeks passed, Izwi found himself adrift in a sea of unfamiliar customs and expectations. He fumbled through village ceremonies, tripping over ancient protocols and struggling to find his place among the people he once called family. The ghosts of his ancestors whispered in his ears, lamenting the loss of a culture that was once so familiar, now strange and alien. His family's homestead stood as a grim reminder of this disconnect.

He stood at the edge of his homestead, gazing out at the ruins of his childhood home. The hut where he had once slept now lay in disrepair, its walls crumbling under the weight of time. A sudden gust of wind stirred the dust, and he saw the eroded remains of his ancestors' graves, their resting places swallowed by the shifting sands of change. As the sun sank below the horizon, Izwi slumped against the wall of his hut, and he caught sight of an old photograph tucked in the corner. It was a picture of Chichi and himself in their youth, their arms wrapped around each other, their smiles bright and full of promise. But time had taken its toll on the image, and a colony of termites had eaten away at Chichi's side of the photo, leaving only Izwi in the frame, frozen in that moment of long-gone joy.

As the shadows of the evening closing in around him, Izwi gazed up at the sky, and for the first time since his return, he saw the twinkling lights of the stars. In the silence of the night, a spark of insight kindled within him. He realized that his journey was not an end, but a beginning—a chance to weave together the past and the present, to stitch the threads of his heritage into a vibrant tapestry of the future. Inspired by the stars that shone overhead, Izwi set to work, rebuilding the ruins of his family's homestead and re-establishing his connection to the land. He tended to the neglected fields, coaxing life from the once-barren soil. The graveyard was a place where Izwi had often come to find solace and connection to his roots. But now, as he stood among the ancestral graves, he felt a piercing loneliness that cut him to the core. The names inscribed on the headstones were familiar to him, the stories of his people woven into his DNA. But the spirits that had once comforted him now seemed distant and cold, the memories of his ancestors fading like echoes in the wind. He restored the graves of his ancestors, placing fresh flowers at their headstones as a sign of respect and remembrance.

Every day, Izwi dug into the earth, seeking to restore the graves of his ancestors and with it, a sense of belonging. But with each stone he turned, he found only more emptiness, more fragments of the past that could not be pieced together. As he stumbled through the ruins of his ancestral homestead, he found the scepter that once held the power of his family's heritage, now gnawed away by rodents and reduced to splinters. The sacred relics that had connected him to his people lay in tatters, devoured by time and neglect. He could feel the weight of his ancestors' disapproval, the disapproving gazes of his village, and the heavy silence of a history he had neglected. Izwi withdrew further into his ruined hut, its walls a testament to the crumbling of his world. He ceased to leave, even for meals, subsisting on whatever scraps he could scavenge from the empty fields. The village fell silent around him, whispers of his downfall carried on the wind, until even the birds seemed to avoid his shadow. He had become a man of sorrow, alone in the wilderness of his heart.

In the silence of his hut, Izwi fell into the routines of despair, like a ritual that eased his mind even as it hardened his heart. He lost track of the days, the hours blurring into each other like the shadows that lengthened across the floor. He listened to the whisper of the wind, the distant chatter of the village, and he wondered if he would ever find his way back to the light. Izwi took refuge in the bottle, its contents numbing his mind and heart. He sat in the shadows of his hut, mumbling to himself, his voice a chorus of anguish and loss. The drink became a companion, a false friend that promised solace but delivered only more pain. Each day he drank, and each day the darkness within him grew, until it seeped from his pores, staining the walls of his hut with the reek of despair. As Izwi's cries pierced the night, the elders gathered outside his hut, their faces etched with concern. They whispered among themselves, wondering what had

143

befallen their once-promising son. They knocked on his door, imploring him to open, to let them in, but Izwi only retreated further into his prison of isolation, unwilling or unable to find the path back to the light. The elders persisted, day after day, bringing food and kind words, offering their guidance and wisdom. But Izwi remained steadfast in his descent, wrapped in a cocoon of self-destruction. The elders became more desperate, beseeching the ancestors for guidance, lighting incense and performing sacred rituals to bring back the man who had once been their pride and joy. Izwi was haunted by visions of the past—his childhood in the village, the love he had shared with Chichi, the future he had once envisioned. He saw the graves of his ancestors, calling out to him, pleading with him to return to the fold. But Izwi could not answer their call, trapped in a prison of his own making. In the depths of his despair, Izwi was visited by a terrible thought—that perhaps his ancestors had abandoned him, that perhaps there was no redemption for him in this world. In his fevered mind, he saw a darkness creeping toward him, a void that threatened to swallow him whole. Izwi rose to his feet, unsteady, as though he were walking on shifting sand. He stumbled toward the door of his hut, the night air chill against his skin. Outside, he saw the stars, cold and distant, uncaring. He stood there, swaying, as the shadows closed in around him, and he heard a voice whispering to him from the depths of his soul, "Let go, my child. Let go."

Chichi reclined on her couch, lost in her life and sipping a glass of red wine. Without paying much attention, she flipped through the channels on her flat-screen TV. Suddenly something familiar rejuvenates her attention, the breaking news and the anchor's grave face. She listened, her heart growing heavier with every word. "A mid-Aged man Izwi Tapera was found in a critical state this evening," he intoned, "following weeks of reported self-isolation." The room grew cold around her. A chill crept up Chichi's spine, the shadows

144

in the room seeming to grow darker, the silence more pronounced. She could feel a tightness in her chest, a knot of pain that threatened to consume her. She thought of the past, of the man loved, now a stranger to himself. She thought of the road not taken, the choices she could not undo. And in that moment, she felt regret wash over her like a cold tide. Tears began to stream down Chichi's cheeks, each drop a tributary of what she had lost, of what she had given up. She tried to fight the feeling, to push it down, but it surged up within her like a tsunami. She clutched her chest, gasping for air, the pain of her betrayal and regret coursing through her veins. She knew that she had made a grave mistake, one that she could never take back, and the realization was crushing her. Chichi sat, motionless, the news still playing in the background. She knew, in that moment, what she had to do. She had to go to Izwi. She had to see him, to apologize, to tell him that she still cared. But what if he rejected her? What if it was too late?

Chichi tore out of the driveway, her car a blur of speed and emotion. The night air whipped through her hair, the wind carrying with it a chorus of regrets. She drove, her hands gripping the steering wheel, her mind a tangle of what-ifs and should-haves. Her foot pressed down on the accelerator, as if she could outrun the pain that pursued her like a relentless hound. Chichi pulled up at Tapera homestead center, where she saw an ambulance parked in front of a circle of onlookers. She fought through the crowd, her heart beating in her throat, until she saw him lying on a stretcher. Her breath caught in her chest as she took in the sight of Izwi, his body ashen and still, he had suffered a severe depression and shock. She rushed to his side, her tears falling on his face as she planted a kiss on his lips. Chichi sat beside Izwi's still form in the ambulance, her hand clutched tightly around his. She could feel the bumpy road, the jostle of the ambulance, and yet she felt as though she were adrift, lost in a sea of emotions. She thought of the night they had first met, of the promises they had made to each other. Chichi kept vigil at Izwi's bedside, her grief a silent sentinel.

As the days passed, she was caught in the net of dread that Izwi's soul would depart, leaving only the shell of his body behind. She imagined the village holding a funeral, and laid Izwi to rest, Chichi could feel the loss not just of only a lost husband, but a part of herself. She felt his absence deep in the faucets of her heart, but in her soul she felt his memory alive in the whispers of the wind and the songs of Izwi's ancestors.

When the weeks passed and Izwi remained in his coma, his family and the village gathered around his bedside, their prayers and hopes buoyed by the flicker of life that still lingered within him. Chichi remained at his side, her vigil an unwavering expression of love. The ancestors whispered their encouragement, their songs of strength echoing through the halls of the hospital. In the depths of his coma, Izwi hovered between the world of life and death, his mind a tangle of memories and desires. He could hear the voices of those he loved, their words swirling around him like a river. He tried to call out to them, to Chichi, his voice a silent scream in the darkness. But the divide between his soul and the physical world was like a vast chasm, separating him from the life he once knew, the life he had turned his back on. But there were other moments when he could feel the presence of those who loved him, the gentle touch of Chichi's hand, the whispered words of his family and the ancestors slowly departing from him. A dread he couldn't barely absorb.

One morning the sun crested over the horizon, a spark of light flickered within him, the promise of a new dawn rising. As the word spread through the village that Izwi was recovering well from his coma, the people gathered outside the homestead, their faces alight with anticipation. The ancestors seemed to join them, their spirits drifting among the trees, the wind a chorus of celebration. Chichi sat at Izwi's bedside, her eyes fixed on his face, waiting for the moment when his eyes would open.

When Izwi opened his eyes, Chichi rejoiced with a face lit up with a smile that could outshine the sun. The whole village erupted into a cacophony of joyous celebration as word spread. Women ululated with glee and children danced in the fields as drums thundered in celebration. The air was alive with the heady scent of smoke from the fire pits and the aroma of roasted maize and goat meat, prepared to welcome their beloved son back to the fold. But joy soon gave way to heartache as days passed by. The man remained lost within himself, they watched him struggle to recall even the simplest of memories. Izwi had been replaced by a stranger. And his life he had once known had been turned upside down.

Even though his memories may have been lost. Advocate Mboko, steadfast in his loyalty and to the preservation of the flourishing business, resolutely devoted himself to the tasks of expanding and defending the Taperas's commercial realm. Chichi and Tariro's love remained stronger than ever before, a beacon of hope in the darkness of Izwi's absentia.

Double Think: War is the New Peace
Rogers Atukunda

War is dirty and ugly. Period. In a split second, it turns a beautiful land into a rotten pigsty. It concerns ruthless and uncouth men regardless of colour, race, nationality or religion whose mission on earth is to stamp out the human species. George Orwell in his book, *Nineteen Eight-Four* (1949), predicts that in our New World; war is the new peace and ignorance is strength.

In his essay titled *"War is Peace; Freedom is Slavery; Ignorance is Strength;"* published on *HumansAreFree.com*, Alexander Light, a blogger, says the three slogans were used by the English Socialist Party ("INGSOC") in Oceania whose goal was "to achieve total control over the citizens and, more importantly, over their minds".

Alexander explains that one of the main mind programs of The Party was the so-called "double thinking", or doublethink, which "describes the act of simultaneously accepting two mutually contradictory beliefs as correct, often in distinct social contexts."
The modern despot will wage wars and manipulate people to believe there is peace. He/She will discourage freedom by convincing the masses that "freedom is slavery". Alexander writes: "Freedom is slavery" is the very foundation of our global society, and the biggest and most ignored problem of a so-called democracy. All human beings are in fact "currency slaves", meaning that they must work to survive (though physical labour could have been abolished by now), but at the same time, almost all of them strongly believe they are free."

Our failed modern democrats discourage rational thinking by telling the people that "ignorance is strength" hence believing without

148

question. "Finally, the strength given by ignorance is highly encouraged in our society: never question authority, law, legal institutions, school books, history, main stream media or main stream scientific communities," notes Alexander.

Alexander applies the Orwellian slogan applied to our modern societies where the concept of "war is peace" is used by the United States of America and North Atlantic Treaty Organization (NATO), when they engage in the so called "pre-emptive wars".

He concludes: "We are both prisoners and prison masters, constantly policing ourselves and each other. And even though we are not aware of it, we are all subjects to carefully designed mind programming, indoctrination and brainwashing, from birth to death."

In this light, any deviation from the socially accepted norm is swiftly fought and corrected by society, with the help of the individuals. Weighing Alexander's words makes me think that when God looks down at us from the compound of his paradise; he holds his sides with mock laughter. He created man with as much simplicity as possible. Man then designed coloured papers and called them "money" plunging societies into mayhem. We have no relationship at all with these papers with graphics on them. When Napoleon Bonaparte [French emperor] said that men are led by toys; he meant the way we worship paper notes. What can't men do to inhale the scent of those papers? These papers mean power. Power! I hate that word.

A Greek philosopher and scientist, Aristotle, in his book, *Nicomachean Ethics* says: "the life of money-making is one undertaken under compulsion, and wealth is evidently not the good we are seeking; for it is merely useful and for the sake of something else.

And so one might rather take the aforenamed objects to be ends; for they are loved for themselves. But it is evident that not even these are ends; yet many arguments have been thrown away in support of them. Let us leave this subject, then."

Useless reasons are fronted for massive manslaughter. Napoleon the Great made himself the dominant figure in Europe. Men, who shared his dream of mastering the world, including Kaiser William and Adolf Hitler of Germany, General Tojo of Japan, General Franco of Spain and Benedicto Mussolini of Italy terrorised the world in the chase for conquest, economic benefits, cultural imperialism and political domination! The cost of these clashes ranges from disease, unemployment, immorality, famine, depression, burning of villages to mass destruction. The world will never forget it's near extermination by militaristic Nazi Hitler and his fascist ally Mussolini. The Japanese will live to tell the holocausts resulting from the atomic bombs dropped on their cities Hiroshima and Nagasaki. Sages believe that the money spent in paying for past wars and preparing for future wars can be put to more constructive use. If those millions are spent in medical research, incurable diseases would cease to exist. More parks, highways, schools, food, better clothing and homes may be made available to more persons. However, dictators have a different approach all together.

"Three cheers for war in general…war alone…puts the stamp of nobility upon the people who have courage to face it," screamed dictator Mussolini while illustrating the spirit of militarism. Historians illustrate the idea of world peace as a dove; leg-chained and grounded by vices of hatred, greed, suspicion and fear. Louis XIV of France and James I of Scotland believed that they were gods in the face of God?

According to historians, the path of a dictator always leaves religion, education, human liberty, national traditions, industry, science, the family life, great art, music and literature-all down-trodden. Most empires were built on conquest, force, trickery and bribery but the main purpose was to amass wealth, obtain political power and spread a particular doctrine. One of such doctrines is the "superiority or Aryanism" of the German and English races that led to two global wars. Charles Darwin believed that "the white race was the first to evolve and hence the most developed", so it was the duty of the white race to dominate other races....

We will take a sample of John Cecil Rhodes, British colonial statesman and financier who wanted to build a British South African Confederation. He wrote, "I contend that we (the British) are the finest first race in the world, and that the more of the world we inhabit, the better it is for the human race." To prove his assertion, the British executed numerous atrocities on South Africans in decades of the fascist Apartheid regime. How could a man like Rhodes who did not know anything about his own history claim to be the master of human history! He should have visited the British public libraries first. There, he would have read about the 1066 Norman and Viking conquest of England. He would later understand that the British are a mixture of Normans, Vikings and Britons, the Scots and Irish. What "fine race" was he talking about then?

Should we say man has no defined path upon which to tread for a better tomorrow? Has man totally no sense of foresight? Like the English poet, William Wordsworth's "Peter Bell", man has proved that he has no vision. Man does not know what he wants and where to go. No matter the scientific and technological advancement, man is a savage at heart. This savagery is at the very core of his existence.

"What a piece of art is man!" wondered Prince Hamlet in the play, Hamlet by William Shakespeare. Who will ever demystify the complexity of the human mind? What for instance shall one say of Adolf Hitler; a man who, in very few years, turned a green world into a rotten stinking gutter!

While chasing his "Aryan race" twisted ideology to prove that the Germans were the finest race on earth, Hitler staged The Holocaust, the genocide of European Jews during World War II. Between 1941 and 1945, Nazi Germany and its collaborators systematically murdered some six million Jews across German-occupied Europe, around two-thirds of Europe's Jewish population. The murders were carried out primarily through mass shootings and poison gas in extermination camps, chiefly Auschwitz-Birkenau, Treblinka, Belzec, Sobibor, and Chełmno in occupied Poland.

In Namibia, Germans executed The Herero and Nama genocide, a campaign of ethnic extermination and collective punishment which was waged against the Herero and the Nama in German South West Africa by the German Empire. It was the first genocide to begin in the 20th century, occurring between 1904 and 1908.
If you regard this subject archaic, think again. The topic concerns both early and modern man in all his callous capacities. If what historians say happened in ancient times were lies, at least I have heard my own share of truth. I have lived to witness atrocities being meted out on innocent people. Serious crimes have been and are still being recorded of rebels, terrorists, suicide bombers, hijackers, kidnappers and assassins. I have had my own fresh encounter with the holocaust of rebel activities and suicide bombing. I will not repeat it here. But if you insist, I shall quickly run through it.

The Allied Defence Force led by Mulezu and Cobra seized Kasese town in Western Uganda in 1998 and burnt shops and cars, raped women and killed hundreds by stabbing, gun butts and shooting. In all my life, I have heard of Joseph Kony, the terror of Northern Uganda and leader of Lord's Resistance Army who chops people's noses, ears, lips and cooks them for the owners to eat. He is famous for ending the idea of virginity in Northern Uganda, creating a new breed of women without breasts and men without testicles (balls) and babies impaled on roasting sticks on road sides. I recall when Rwandese and Ugandan soldiers slaughtered each other in Katanga and Kisangani in 1998 in the mineral-rich Democratic Republic of Congo. I saw the army trucks pass by on my way to school as they delivered corpses like mails to each doorstep of dumbfounded parents.

My father always brought home newspapers filled with this information. I also read about how Saddam Hussein almost erased Kuwait off the Map of Asia in 1991 and then hewed off the Iranian president's head. Historians say that Americans trained Osama to terrorise the Arabic world but at all times, wickedness turns out to be self-defeating. If it is true that they trained him for terrorism, (attacking and inflicting pain on innocent people), then they were great teachers for he succeeded in blasting the Pentagon and killing hundreds of innocent people as the mission instructed. It was not new since Americans had earlier on mulched the Vietnamese and Chinese in rice fields like thatch grass. They still proudly idolise their onslaughts in commando films. They again plundered and looted Iraq in 2003, recently marauded and looted Libya and may soon do the same in Iran and North Korea.

These conditions seem to suggest the coming of World War III. The advancement in science and technology should be wholeheartedly

153

embraced for modernisation and development purposes-but in the industrial, agricultural, scientific and educational sectors not just the militia. The implication of initiating modern weapons like nuclear bombs, missiles, fighter planes, steamer warships, atomic or poison gas, rocket launchers and others; is that it creates insecurity hence sparking an arms race. My history teacher constantly emphasized that weapons are always designed for war but not decorations for parties. Then countries in the pretext of testing their new weapons start confronting each other and before you know it, a global war is upon our heads.

I hope this is the prophesied time when man shall be civilised enough to be ashamed of wars. War is not a feast where people go to enjoy; it is a pit full of fire out of which few escape with un-burnt hair. If animals, birds and insects that have a smaller brain no longer fight over mates, what's wrong with the higher life humans? We all cry for peace, love and harmony but we should be the initiates of these ideals. To paraphrase Mahatma Gandhi's words, "we should be the change we want to see in the world and cultivate the spirit of dying without killing". We all know that happiness is the most important thing in human life, what have we done to establish it? We all fear dying but we continue to kill others. I agree with those who believe that "the future should be made a golden age of peace and progress". But how is this possible in a world crafted out of greed, malice and avarice?

For the case of American imperialism and aggression, the title super power is like any other title and it always changes hands. Always! It's no man's property and no one can claim an eternal right to it. I am not old enough to give lectures about humanity but the history I have read has taught me that fact. There was a time when the word "Rome" meant the very existence of the world. A time when your tongue would swiftly be cut out for misspelling that word! Latin was the language of the educated, the high class or the gifted medics of the time but now, it is a fossilized language. What happened? Our super ego can always swell and over swell but life shall stay larger than us.

If you brand someone a dictator, accuse him of oppressing the citizens and manufacturing nuclear weapons (which of course you have and are the lead in producing), then attack him without permission from United Nations (UN), since you are UN, destroy state and private property, murder his family, friends, relatives and anyone associated with the leader, brutally execute the national army and hang the leader like a sack of sorghum; are you still bleating about peace? By the way, if you came to bring democracy and freedom, why then are you hurriedly carting away national resources casting quick glances over your shoulder? What does an American oil pipeline, which comes first before the new constitution in the plundered state, symbolize in matters of democracy?

I had prepared solutions like need for diplomatic relations, intimacy and divine consideration, civilization of the mind, soul and body, blah, blah but I later dismissed them as a drunkard's babble. We have heard this gibberish before and the world has continued to rot the more. I will leave the idea of the world as "a global village" for idealists and daydreamers. Some historian believes that: "the limitation of armaments, the acceptance of arbitration as the natural solvent of international disputes, the reflection of wars of ambition and aggression to the categories of absolete follies: these will be the milestones which mark the stages of the road".

Albert Einstein (published 1934) believes that, "Anybody who really wants to abolish war must resolutely declare himself in favour of his own country's resigning a portion of its sovereignty in favour of international institutions: he must be ready to make his own country amenable, in case of a dispute, to the award of an international court. He must, in the most uncompromising fashion, support disarmament all round, as is actually envisaged in the unfortunate Treaty of Versailles; unless military and aggressively patriotic education is abolished, we can hope for no progress."

Well, I strongly believe that such is what will always happen if the world continues begetting pig-headed dictators and global looters and plunderers. I am putting blame on the world because, like Richard Wright's hero, Bigger Thomas, these despots are all native sons. If garbage can insist on breeding remorseless brutal bullies and if streets persist on harbouring ruthless hoodlums; such are the tragic mishaps that will always strangle humanity.

Adapted from "Multi-Continental Affair" by Rogers Atukunda, BA Literature/English Makerere University, Kampala-Uganda.

FOOD FOR THOUGHT

Christopher Kudyahakudadirwe

"Sekuru, if you don't do something for us now, you better start digging there!" Ambuya announced in a weak voice pointing at the headstones of our children's graves jutting out of an anthill a stone's throw away from our home.

I looked at her. She was a youthful wife whose beauty hadn't been touched by the famine that gripped the land. She had lost weight like everybody else who didn't have enough to eat; her face weathered, wilting like an uprooted flame lily. Our three grandchildren lay next to the dying fire like abandoned bundles, their eyes moons of destitution, their bodies wasting away before my eyes. All our cows and goats had long died.

The president and the ruling party accused El Nino and the West of causing the drought despite the rain dances and the libations we poured on the ground for a bountiful season. Our chests sighed with relief when he declared it a national disaster. We knew that anything labelled 'national disaster' meant the government had a responsibility to look after us.

My eyes misted when I looked at my wife again, I only saw a shadow of what she had been in better times. The woman had been a pillar to lean on since I came from the bush after demobilisation. The war ended when she was thirteen years old, and I married her two years later when I was seconded to the 4.3 Reserve Battalion in the new army stationed in the southern province. Then life was sweet and we were young, what with the army salary and a pension which we lost later, we managed to build this house as well as send our children to school. Now all our children died of COVID-19 at its peak in 2020 leaving behind three grandchildren to look after.

For the past two days, we hadn't eaten anything, and I couldn't just continue looking at my family starving. I had to do something, I said to myself, something to rescue them from starvation. Fellow villagers had ostracised us for supporting the young man from the opposition party who opposed the old man from the ruling party during the August election. The councillor denied us a share of the government food assistance even after the president declared on television that no citizen would die of hunger.

I had to do something, I said to myself again as I stood beside the road from the city. I had no idea what I had to do. I looked up at the blue sky, it had no suggestions for me. I looked at the trees, but they ignored me choosing to rustle their leaves instead. Only the sun made a blazing suggestion.

The sun blazed hot; heat waves rose from the road surface the way petrol fumes do from an open container. Images in the middle distance danced like reflections on a disturbed water surface. Brown dry scrub bush, with baobab trees sticking like giants in a fairy tale challenged the prolonged drought. I braved the hot sun as I waited, waiting for nothing in particular, while thirst assaulted my throat and a protest brewed in my stomach. Small bugs whined at my ears, making me slap myself as I tried to swat them dead.

When I walked away from home that morning, I had no idea where I was going to and what I was going to do there. Ambuya's words echoed in my mind as they accompanied me on my way to nowhere. I weaved through the scorched knee-high maize plants so dry I could light them with a match. I walked with hunger growling in my tummy like a caged angry leopard. I walked away from the only place I was welcome not knowing whether I would be back at all. I walked away.

Of course, I had to do something; I was the man of the house. At that time, I began to regret the side of politics I had identified with during the run-up to the previous election when the charismatic

158

young leader of the opposition convinced many people that the time for the removal of the ruling party was now or never. Many comrades stood with the young man because he promised us a better life, better than what we received from the ruling party for the past forty-four years it was in government. We began to dream again. We began to dream the way we dreamed during chimurenga.

Yes, I had to do something, but the question was what was that something that I had to do?

My comrades accused me of abandoning the ruling party. They said that I had become a sell-out, a puppet of the West, enjoying the crumbs from the imperialists' tables, so I didn't deserve the food provided by the government I was against. I was biting the hand that giveth, they said. They didn't care that I was at the war front during the chimurenga with them; they forgot that I had scars from fighting for the one-man-one-vote and equality. They don't remember the torture that we endured at the hands of the settler soldiers; they don't remember the sacrifices we had to bear as we faced buffalo beans, snakes and wild beasts in the valleys and forests of the motherland; they don't remember the lice and ticks we endured in the bush. They remember nothing at all. Is forty-four years such a long time for them to forget our ordeal?

At sixty-five I retired, but my pension had been eroded by inflation. In 1997, I remember, we booed the late former president at the Heroes Acre and beat drums and sang war songs drowning his speech; he immediately offered us fifty thousand dollars each for our contribution to the chimurenga. That money was immediately eroded by the inflation that followed soon after this doling of the money. With it, I bought a small tractor and a plough the 'carcass' of which was rusting in the rain and the sun at the back of my falling-apart house. I didn't plough an acre with it because, without knowledge of how a tractor works, I drove it without water, and it

159

blew the gasket. There was no money to take the engine to the engineers in the city nor to hire a mechanic to do that for me.

I looked around. The trees lining the steep roadside cast their shade to give me relief from the scorching sun. I happened to look at the edge of the road and there, where the tarmac and the drying grass merged I saw some grains of yellow maize that must have dropped from the lorries carrying relief grain to the villages further to the north of the district. I went down on my knees and started picking up the grains one by one hoping to gather enough to roast in a pan and feed my grandchildren. It was a tedious job to do, but I continued to do it.

Perhaps that was what I had to do.

Then I heard the convoy of lorries labouring up the incline which would let them roll down the slope to the river from which they would start the sharp climb up the steep slope to where I was busy picking up the maize grains. These grains were my last hope to feed the people back home. I didn't want to lose any of those people.

So, this was *something* that I had to do.

I remembered how the words of the ruling party's secretary for information and publicity foretold what was coming. Just by seeing things differently from my comrades, I had become an enemy, an undesirable rabble to be starved. The news from the Middle East had stories of food being used as a weapon to starve some people within the same borders. Yes, I heard most of my news on the small solar-powered radio I received from the opposition party I joined a few months before the elections. Was this not the same as what was going on around me? I paused and looked around as if the answer hid in the branches of the trees hanging above the road.

Then I remembered that the previous day the ruling party councillor had come through our village announcing that lorries with grain would be coming to the growth point five kilometres to the north and people should bring their party cards to receive their share.

160

I had publicly burnt my ruling party card at a meeting when the opposition held its first rally at the same growth point in June last year.

I did something.

As I thought about the day I struck a match and torched my ruling party card, I heard the lorries bellowing up the first steep slope to the growth point. Soon I saw the head of the first lorry bobbing up as it crossed the bridge. I could see the bags of maize in the trailer, they were not covered with a tent. What was in those bags was what I was squatting here to pick at the roadside, I thought to myself. A long time ago when we were in a camp in the neighbouring country, food ran out and the rationing introduced meant receiving a handful of boiled maize grains for the day. We survived on roots, we were not allowed to shoot the impalas and buffaloes that roamed the forest where our camp was hidden.

One day my friend said, "If we don't do something we'll starve to death. Let's ask for deployment at the battlefront. The povo will feed us. It's better to die while your stomach is full."

"Why don't we just run away from this camp and join any group of comrades we'll meet at the battlefront," I said.

So we did something.

The leading lorry thundered past where I stood leaving me engulfed in the wind in its wake. My eyes followed its cargo wishing one bag to accidentally drop without the driver noticing and then I would go with it to drive away the hunger that crouched at my doorstep back home. But such fortuitous moments never happen in real life. However, I realised something as the lorry went past: some branches of the trees were almost scratching the lorry's top. I remembered how my uncle, the brother of my mother, told us that he used to pick crates of drinks from bus racks as the buses drove under a tree branch on which he would be lying.

I had to do something.

161

The second lorry laboured up the steep inclination as I climbed the tree whose branch extended above the road. While I was up there I realised that there were three lorries and that it was best to ambush the last one so that I don't have to rush coming down from the tree to salvage my loot. As old as I was I didn't feel any shame about what I intended to do. I was still strong enough to pick a fifty-kg bag of maize and let it drop on the road. After all who wasn't looting from the government? I had to do something to save my family like what my friend and I did almost half a century ago to save ourselves.

So, the third and last lorry came up the road slowly. I adjusted my position accordingly and waited. From my position, I could see the driver, but he did not see me. He wiped his sweating torso with a towel that hung around his neck. I could see that his eyes were fixed on the road. I wondered what was going through his mind. Just then the cab of the lorry was under the branch and then the trailer. Without wasting time, I grabbed the corners of one bag with all my strength. Time slowed down as I waited for the trailer of the lorry to pass under me while the bag slipped on top of other bags. As soon as the trailer drove away, I dropped the bag onto the road. I quickly descended from the tree and hauled the bag onto my shoulder and disappeared into the brown scrub. I didn't want anyone to see me with the bag of maize on my back so I went deep into the bush and waited for the sun to set.

"That's what your comrades do to survive," Ambuya told me. "But then you're not stealing any gold or diamonds like what those up there do." She pointed a finger towards the roof, smiled and said, "Now Sekuru did something."

That was food for thought. The pot on the fire boiled over; the smell of sadza filled the hut. Ambuya added a little more mealie meal to thicken it.

We all smiled.

Me and the Dudes
Natisha P. Parsons

A Personal Word to the Reader

A man's rights, and education begin in the home. If he lacks the necessary foundations, he is likely to build on nothing of worth. Too many a man, today seems to believe that he can thrash his wife with his whip when he feels like it. Domestic violence should not exist. This writer can tell a personal story or two from personal experience. This story is about boys who could give grown men readers some insight into where things went wrong in their own lives and make amends if possible. It's hard to fathom just how the love of your life turned out to become the nightmare you never believed would happen to you. Children who read this story can identify themes endured in their present lives and make amends if possible. Even women could glean a thing or two from this story, and make amends where possible. This writer's teaching years exposed her to a large variety of home backgrounds to which children are exposed.

This writer had an encounter with the Lord Jesus Christ when she was 45 years old and wished passionately that she'd been born again at a much earlier age. Evil is real and we live in a world that is fraught with evil and she can swear to it that there would be no evil in this world if everyone had a living relationship with their Creator. He is very real and He is not a religion. He proved it when He became a man and came to supply the answer to evil and its stronghold on humanity. He took God's wrath on behalf of Believers,

This is not a religious story nor is it a sermon by any stretch of the imagination. Unconditional love for humanity is one of this writer's blessings from her Creator upon establishment with Him. It should be noted that Heaven and Hell are real eternal destinies for mankind. God sends no one to hell. The onus has been placed on mankind to make the choice which is not hard at all. This writer can testify to that. Its everyone's right to have the correct foundational upbringing.

Part 1

I am Peter-John, PJ for short. I have a very strict mother and I love her like you won't understand. My dad passed away and she has been Mum and Dad rolled into one. She speaks to me about upholding the family name constantly. I am careful to do nothing that will disgrace the name. Disappointing Mom is no option. I keep no secrets from her, if I can help it. She is a committed Christian and has, written up behind the bathroom door, and covered in plastic:

Don't fail to discipline your children. They won't die if you spank them. Physical discipline may well save them from death Proverbs 23: 13&14.

I have had one experience of this obedience on Mom's part and I am very careful not to come in for a repeat performance. I don't remember who cried more – Mom or me. I remember that I had deserved every lash that fell on my squirming behind. I dare not deny it. If I had thought about it, I wouldn't have taken that money… who else could it possibly be when Mom and I lived alone? I had the boldness to buy her a bar of milk chocolate, telling her I had picked up the hundred-rand note in the grass along the short cut from the taxi rank. When she went for her purse to send me to the café for bread and the paper, she knew exactly where I had "picked up" the one hundred-rand note. When she called me to her bedroom in '*that*' voice, I knew the game was up! I ran into her room and threw my arms around her, squeezing tightly, crying like a whipped puppy. I laugh when I recall that day.

She left me to cry and then held me away from her. She reached over and pulled up a bunch of tissues from her dressing table and mopped me up so tenderly, I thought I was in the clear… forgiven…

"What's making my baby cry like this?" she caught me by the chin and looked into my eyes, then kissed me loudly on the forehead.

"I-I-I ...'m so-so-sorry, Mom. I won't do it again," I was blubbering; my nose was out of order, so she handed me some tissues.

She actually took me by the shoulders and held me away from her. "What has my precious boy done that he's sorry for?" And she kissed my forehead again. I thought Mom knew what I was sorry for, but it looked like I was wrong. What was she calling me for in '*that voice*'?

To make matters worse, she tugged me close and hugged me tightly, kissing me on the top of my head. When I felt a wetness fall on the back of my neck, I pulled back and looked up at her. Mom was crying! Shocked I stared at her and she said, "Oh my baby. I just can't believe you did this." Her voice got louder as she spoke. Then she was howling like she was being spanked. I just stood there staring at her. I didn't remember seeing her cry.

Mom got to her feet and took me by the hand. She gave me a talk that I will always remember. She spoke about the people in jail that were once little boys and girls their parents were proud of. Small things children steal and get away with encourage them to get more and more daring until they become so good at it, and enjoy the victory so much, they eventually become criminals and even kill people who get in their way. She spoke in such a way, the pictures I was able to see in my mind made what she said unforgettable.

Briskly she strode outside and picked a switch from the quince tree. What happened next is best forgotten. I was in Grade Two then. I have never taken even a pencil that didn't belong to me. I see my mother's eyes looking at me and crying her eyes out because her little boy had stolen.

"It's not the thing you steal," she says, "Its stealing... thievery... *it's a sin!*" I made up my mind I will not be a thief. My memories did

165

not entertain me. I still feel lousy when I remember opening that purse and planning my story. I can't, try as hard as I may, remember what I bought with that money apart from the chocolate bar, of course. Mom still keeps that chocolate bar as a reminder that her little boy thought of her even when he was doing wrong. It was a sign that he was feeling bad about what he'd done and hoped the chocolate would be a sort of bandage over the sore.

Now, some years later, on this afternoon, I was all on my own. It was the July holiday. The sun was shining, and birds were noisily enjoying the sky. Obviously, there were fish to dive for. I wanted pictures of diving sea birds for my scrap book. Living close to the ocean is wonderful. I love it.

I hear about peer pressure all the time from my schoolteacher mother. She reminds me often enough that the worst, most hardened criminals were once upon a time the cutest little bundle that the stork ever left on their parent's doorstep.

Misbehaviour would have me and The Corporal (short for Corporal Punishment) visiting with her in her bedroom and I was not going to invite that at all. The Corporal was a shop-bought replacement for the quince switch. Will I ever forget that day?! No peer pressure was going to get me to Mom's bedroom with the Corporal. Every time I caught sight of The Corporal, *Don't fail to discipline your children...* would flash across my mind. She made me learn it by heart, back then.

I'd've jumped right back into bed if I knew what the day held. Such a beautiful day with so much bad in it!

The fishermen would be laughing, though.

I rushed through my wash and brush up, nuked last night's left-over curried cabbage, sausage, and roti (yum!) and scooted out to meet the day. Perhaps I'd go watch the fishermen down at the pier.

No point saying *Ciao, Ma*. She wouldn't appreciate being disturbed. I like that Italian greeting.

Hopping and skipping; whistling, and whooping, kicking at the odd stone, I jogged along, happy as a cat with mouse and cream! I had no special plans, except thinking of going to the pier. For some reason, I thought of what Gran used to say: "The devil always finds work for idle hands!" Mom's favourite was: " What you do in the dark, WILL come out in the light." Mrs Brown, another widow down the road, was often heard screaming at her bunch: "Beware... your sins WILL find you out!" She said it with a scary shiver in her voice that made it feel like a million little legs were crawling over my back and head.

I hoped the devil would find no work for my idle hands. I'd maybe go help one of the old men down at the pier. A boy can learn a lot from the old fishermen.

Mrs Brown has five naughty sons none of us like to play with. Now they call me "the nasty geek" and we ignore each other. Tommy is tall, fifteen, and in Grade 7 with his two younger brothers Gary and Bart. Patrick and Werner are in Grade two. Tommy picked on me one day and we met to sort it out.

That was the day I was in a real knock-down, drag-out *fight*. I am a peaceful kind of chap. I laugh off many things other boys shape up for. And that was when Tommy Brown's attack pounced on me like a cat on an unsuspecting rat. He pulled a mad-dog-snarl face at me and growled and said, "Hoppy, Hoppy, Half Leg." And that wasn't all...

I saw red.

I was grateful for the boxing lessons I had been taking since I was six years old. My friends, The Boys, gave his brothers no chance to pack me. My shares rose high that day because The Dudes didn't know "I had it in me".

"Hey, PJ, I never know you can fight, bro."

167

"Check the guy... not even one teeny, tiny, little bruise."

"Check out poor ole Tommy... *two* globes!"

"Tomorrow he's gonna be a sorry sight."

"*If* he remembers to bath, he'll be on fire."

The comments flew around me, but my mind was a mess!

"What will Mom say?"

"She thinks fighting is for guttersnipes..."

"Maybe I am *a guttersnipe?"*

I was like on autopilot. Fighting is just not my beat. The rest of the day passed in a kind of unreal blur. I pretended to be hundreds.

It was hectic! My hyper friends banged my back and mussed up my hair. It was also funny. "Re-e-e-e-*treat!*" Sakkie yelled after the Brown boys. "*Hup*, two, three, four..." His father was in the army and he knew some stuff. The whistles and comments that followed the howling, swearing Tommy and his howling, swearing brothers made me feel really lousy. I dreaded facing his mother and mine for an explanation of his bloodied nose and ... yikes!! ...*those eyes!* I shuddered. Mom would tell Pastor Roberts before he heard it from TTD ("The Township Daily"). I would have to tell the truth and that sounded lame!

I have one short leg that causes me to sort of hop when I walk. This boy called me Hoppy and I saw red. I was raised to be hardened to ugly words because Mom said children can be cruel and I should accept that I have this condition. "You have this short leg and it's here to stay. Accept it. You were born like that. If people say mean things, look at them and ask them *what's new?*"

I have never been bothered by the teasing I get because those words don't trouble me at all. Like Mom said, this leg is here to stay. But on that day, when the school bully teased me, I really got mad. To crown matters he also called me by a name I really resent.

Tommy drew closer and muttered, "amper baas" (Afrikaans - almost white) and that was the red flag! My temper skyrocketed!

168

"Amper baas" is *really* nasty and *horribly, insultingly* derogatory… big time! It's not my fault that I was born so white. Not quite albino but the closest thing. Even my eyebrows and eyelashes are white but my eyesight's okay. I'd not refuse *that* invitation to the usual place and time where scores were settled. I could *smell* the fight, not dreaming I could be beaten up silly by the bigger boy.

After the fight I was snatched up and shouldered off to the café for a coke. I thought I'd make them feel good, so I put on an act when we got there. I swaggered ahead of them… came to a stop, half turned with one hand on my hip, cocked an imaginary cap and said in my best throaty, American cowboy drawl: "Make mine a Sprite, boys." Then I lifted my short leg, wiggled it a few times and gave one of my awful squashed-up-face winks. That had them shrieking and imitating, and then calling out their own preferences until the shop assistant shouted HEY, HEY, HEY, THIS ISN'T THE SOCCER GROUNDS.

"Great Pretender" – one of my late gramps' favourite songs – was playing on the radio. *Great Pretender – that's me.* Memories flashed by that made me feel even worse about the fight. *Why didn't I just ignore him*???

"Celebrations," shouted Sakkie, only he said 'cereblations'. "Our PJ beat that big bully in Grade seven!"

"No! You mean that *beeeg* Brown boy?" The assistant's eyes went wide.

"The same," someone shouted. The yell went up again and fists boxed the air.

"AWRAAIT, AWRAAIT," she screamed. "Pipe down. Free drinks for all of you. Place your orders. I'll pay for them. It's long that boy been bullying my Christopher. Now I know how to stop it." We grabbed our cans and left before she changed her mind.

Tommy's bullying stopped. I heard that he was threatened with me – *Bulldog PJ*. What a laugh. I'm not the fighting type…really.

Amper baas! What an insult! People of all colours live nicely together in Jabu. We're all colour-blind. There's a lot of crime, but we have our tactics: burglar bars, padlocks, vicious dogs, and leave-nothing-valuable-outside. Some people even have guns and large heavy grass-cutting knives called pangas. On TV I heard them being called machetes in some country.

The Dudes never included me in their daring adventures. My mom would kill me if she knew what they got up to. I didn't say it out loud, but they were practicing criminals! It never occurred to them to simply cut me out of their lives. Actually, we got on well together, playing TV, board, and card games especially on rainy days, and during holidays. Also, I was no fool on the soccer field! They also respected my "non-operational" fists. Got that word from Sakkie. Sakkie spoke fluent Zulu. His home language was Afrikaans and sometimes his English was hard to follow.

Suddenly my thoughts were rudely interrupted. "*Peter-Jo- - -hn… PJ-a-a-ay…*" Only Sapho could shriek that shrilly and that loudly. I turned. Walking backwards, I shouted, "*Ja?*"

He ran to catch up with me.

"Where you off to?" he asked.

"Nowhere in particular," I answered. "Where you going?"

"Lucky's… long list. Come with?"

"Sure. Mom's still in bed. Saturday… you know the story."

"Of course, your mama's day off. We depend on Dad's Friday night wages. You guys shop monthly and top up Fridays."

"Yep!"

"Race you," shouted Saps, speeding off.

"No fair. You got a start." I sped off not having a hope of beating him. He was the star sprinter of the school.

Sapho was one of The Dudes but I didn't think he'd pull any tricks. Sapho, Sakkie, Mandla, Harry, Temba and Marcel were The Dudes. They mainly operated at night. Usually, when they started to talk and it sounded like a scary fishy affair, I'd raise my hands and say, "I'm outa here." Temba was really funny. He'd point at me two-gun style and say, "*He-e-e's* outa here."

They were really daring! What if they landed in jail? It made me feel sick to think of it. They'd really suffer there! Marcel and Mandla were altar boys, for crying out loud! The priest would freak! Whiskers! I often wondered what they told him in confession. Did they confess the same sins every time they went there? And that was every Saturday morning.

Saps was a careful shopper. He compared prices, checked cans for dents, and pushed aside crushed packaging and tacky bottles. When I commented, he looked at me, eyebrows raised, and said in a slow, deep voice, "Experience, my deah." We burst out laughing and that got the attention of a security guard.

"Whatchu boys up to? Stealing, hey? Come, lemme check y'alls pockets."

"Not a chance. You not putting *your* hands in *my* pockets!" Another red flag!

"Don't be rude to her," Sapho hissed. "She'll get us in the township. She's new here."

"Oh yeah?" I hissed back. "I'm not allowed to laugh? Laughing means I'm stealing?"

I turned on her. "We are NOT thieves. If you want to search us, you better send for the police and our parents first."

"What's going on here?" a gruff voice demanded. It was the manager.

"Search those boys," our accuser shouted.

People stopped to stare.

Eyeballs!

171

I gave her a dirty look. *Lucky you're a girl*, I thought feeling as vicious as Rintin snarling at strangers.

The manager pulled her aside and they whispered together. Sapho turned to run and I grabbed him by the sleeve. "Wait!" I hissed at him. I was mad as a snake.

Before the manager could open his mouth, I said: "Our parents' spend their hard-earned money here every week, Sir. Before you disgrace us, I want the police and our parents here. I…we…have been badly insulted. Also, I don't think we will be shopping here again."

The manager looked at the security lady; she was giving us the evil eye. He turned back and said, "She's new with us and still has to get to know the faces of all the children around here. We do have lots of trouble with shoplifting and the main culprits are young boys like you. Allow me to apologise for the embarrassment you have suffered. I hope it never happens again."

He looked at her. She looked at the floor. The manager tapped her arm. She looked at us and apologised with a nasty smile. It made me think of the smile the spider must have given the fly, in the poem where he invites her into his parlour.

"That's okay…for now." I kind of smiled too, and nudged Sapho in the ribs. He nodded rapidly. "Yes, me too," he blurted out turning deep red. I burst out laughing. I couldn't help myself. He looked… scared? Sapho? Funny that.

We finished what we had come to do, passed through the check-out and I picked up some of his parcels and we left.

"Yo! PJ! You got guts. I wouldn't be able to choon that toppie like that." (talk to… grownup man)

"I *hate* being accused of stealing."

We were silent the rest of the way.

At last we were hauling the groceries onto their kitchen table.

"Whew!" he let out a big breath of sheer relief. "That was a narrow escape! Thank you, my pal. You did me the biggest favour today"

"Hey? I did?" I was quite puzzled. "Escape? Fro-o-o-o-o-m..."

My eyes widened and my jaw dropped. With a wicked smirk on his face, Sapho took from his pocket, and swung slowly from his fingers, a beautiful black and blue, *expensive* underwater watch

"You're good." I thought, horrified. "You're jolly good!"

Lifting my hands, and shaking my head, I backtracked as if a wasp had stung me. "I'm outta here." My mouth was dry and my breathing too fast.

Was I an accomplice? Did I just aid and abet a crime? Is there such a thing as an unknowing accomplice? Should I do anything? *What a thing*, I told myself, *in future I know what to be on the look-out for.*

I know now what it means to feel *really* lousy.

Part 2

It was still early so I decided to fetch my camera and go down to the pier. Mom was still in bed reading her magazines and filling in her favourite Sudoku puzzles. She was an addict. She gave me money for a movie and a take-away lunch and I was 'A' for away.

"If I do' wanna go see a movie?" I asked.

"It's yours, PJ – spend it as you like."

"A few bottles of beer..." she leaned over and threw a slipper at me. I caught it and put it back near the other one, laughing gayly.

"Don't even make jokes about it. Half the world is swaying about in a drunken stupor and..."

"Ok, Ok, Ma, I know the story. You know I'm joking."

She gave me '*a look*' and went back to her precious Sudoku.

"Movies, bye-bye... pier, many happy returns," I sang aloud as I scooted out the gate. I was keen to use my new camera. It could zoom in and zoom out and even take videos. I imagined I'd be able to take some great videos of madly excited fishermen as they pulled in their tight lines.

I headed for the bush and the short cut that led to the beach and the fishing pier.

I was an aeroplane with sound effects and flew along the badly bumpy path, making sure to keep my eyes on the ground. *Flapping fishing lines*!! So many furrows and so deep! Some with muddy water. Yuck! Gross! Running and jumping, the journey soon ended. Ah-h-h... at last... tar. Because of my short leg my hip sometimes gets sore if I run too much over rough ground with too many lumps and bumps. My hip was sore but not unbearable. I hobbled across the tar road and onto the beach.

The fishing area had all a fisherman would need: concrete benches and tables, taps, huge metal bins lined with big, black plastic bags and the ground was smooth with shiny grey cement. The solidly built wooden pier led off from there.

Puffing and panting, I flopped onto a concrete bench. My heart sank. Just two men on the pier. Suddenly I heard a welcome sound...the ice cream truck. Happiness. I could always think better with an ice cream cone in my hand. I sprinted up the steps.

"How's it, Hoppy?" the ice cream man shouted as he watched me.

"Great," I shouted back. "You know my usual." I'm sometimes called Hoppy or Hop-a-long and I don't mind at all. It makes no difference to me; my leg still stays short.

And soon, joyful-joyful... I was in ice cream heaven. I love the stuff.

Settling back, pleased as can be, I bit the pointed tip of chocolate coating off so I could suck the delicious vanilla-flavoured ice-cream up. I gazed out to sea. The sea gulls squawking and squabbling over

174

food made me grin. A plane flew by in the distance. No ships on the horizon today. My heart leapt when a lonely dolphin jumped up and splashed down again... then another, and another... then more of them... what a treat. Forgotten was my zooming camera. A school of them swam swiftly by leaping and jumping joyfully, just plain showing off, I swear.

I was so enchanted by what I was seeing, with delish ice-cream in my mouth, I joyfully sang out an old Sunday school song, "*All things bright and beautiful...*" My off-key voice would frighten away those bright and beautiful things, if they heard me. I laughed at the thought, almost chocking.

Then my joy was rudely chased away. I closed my eyes and sighed. That morning's happening gnawed at me like rats in the ceiling. One part of me took in and really enjoyed all that was around me, but another dwelt on my part in a robbery.

Then my roving eyes settled on the raised look-out point. It was deserted. From up there I'd see further and better. When I swallowed my last bit of cone, I monkeyed up those steel steps as fast as anyone with two good legs. *Much better view from up here*, I thought.

Suddenly a new sound disturbed my thoughts... a motor boat. I looked up. There it was – a smart blue and white striped motor boat with two men in it. The name Alma was painted across the hull in very fancy blue and orange letters. They were heading for the beach almost directly under me. I imagined a ride across the waves and risked asking them for a short ride... should I ... shouldn't I .... I watched them drag their boat onto the beach.

The two fishermen on the pier went into action. They left their rods flat on the board walk where they were standing and raced down the steps carrying their fishing bags. I watched curiously. I suddenly perked up and remembered...

"Camera!" my mind shouted. I made a rude impatient sound at myself for forgetting to video the fishing birds and diving dolphins.

I set my camera on video. Slowly I zoomed in closer and began to roll.

I was Leon Shuster. No-o-o, I was Walt Disney. Ya-a-a-y. I smiled my birthday smile. Those men were Disney characters. The fishermen were Goofy and Duffy, and the boat men were Mickey and Lumpjaw.

Happily, I let the video run, noticing things about the men. Lumpjaw's belly stood out there. Goofy, Duffy and Mickey were younger and not fat at all. They could have been Lumpjaw's sons. I made up my own little story as I videoed, imagination running wild. They all wore scruffy looking blue denim jeans and different coloured Tees. They had on caps with the brim round the back. The fat man also had a fairly large white hanky under his cap that hung down his back and over his forehead.

Suddenly things took a nasty turn. Lumpjaw and Mickey had taken the bags from the fishermen, checked the contents and nodded their heads. Then Lumpjaw took both bags and went back to the boat. He lifted a bulging briefcase and opened it. My eyes flew open. He lifted out a gun! Revolver, pistol… I don't know the difference. To me a gun is a gun and it's used for one thing. My heart drummed and my hands shook. His gun had a silencer! I recognised it from television. From where I was, I could see exactly what he was doing. And I got it all on video.

I heard the pop-pop-pop as he shot the three men. They sank to the ground as they were shot. They'd tried to get away but failed. Lumpjaw was quick on the draw.

I froze. I couldn't believe my eyes and ears. The video kept rolling. Suddenly, without planning to, I screamed one long terrified scream. This was murder I was witnessing – real life murder, not a crime movie or a documentary – no special effects and such – this was real. Those men were standing up, alive a few seconds ago!

Now murder in our township happened often enough. There were funerals almost every weekend. Too many of them were not natural. But to witness three men being shot down just like that was too much for me.

Lumpjaw looked up. He froze. For a few seconds he just stared at me, open-mouthed. Then he pointed the gun at me. I heard the bullet ping off the underside of the orange coloured hard steel platform I was standing on. My body went cold and shaky. The vibration and the pinging echo went right through me. Even in my tortured mind, the word 'reverberation' flashed briefly.

ACTION! My mind screamed. I don't know how I scaled down those steps without being shot or without toppling down headfirst. When he screamed, swearing vilely, I knew he was out of bullets. The thought brought small relief.

I ran like the devil himself was after me.

"Hey, boy, bring that camera here," he screamed. He flung the gun into the boat and came after me. I was grateful that he was fat and older. I made for the short cut. I'd find a hiding place. I dared not run home – I could not take trouble into my mother's house.

Behind me Lumpjaw, who I renamed Killer, was puffing and panting and shouting, *"Stop thief! Help! Catch that boy. Help! My camera!"*

Liar!

People were walking towards the pier from different directions. The parking area, way to my right, was filling. Tourists with their cameras, families, excited children and more excited dogs seemed suddenly to swarm the place. They were all headed for the pier benches and the look-out points and the picnicking spots on the beaches further along from the pier.

The roadside vendors were busy setting up shop. They were spreading their many different wares on brightly coloured mats. They looked up but ignored the screaming man. People looked at me and

177

simply looked away again. They didn't want to get involved. A beachfront police car passed slowly by and Killer slowed down. He should've asked them to catch me, shouldn't he? Maybe the people milling around thought that, too. I continued running. He wouldn't dare stop them; I knew that.

I came to the short cut turnoff and instead of keeping to the path, I went into the bush and looked for a tree to climb. *Please, let the monkeys be at another spot today*, I prayed. Weaving my way between the branches, bushes, and shrubs, I dared not slow down.

This time I was Hop-a-long Cassidy... no, I was a Russian spy with James Bond after me. I dare not be caught. They would torture my country's precious secrets out of me!

My chest was burning something awful. I was feeling sorry for my own lungs.

"The money and the boat," rattled in my head. "He's *gotta* go back there." Poor criminal. Thieves were everywhere. Would the money mean anything if the camera got into the hands of the police? He had a hard decision: catch me or save his money. He needed to do both.

Painfully huffing and puffing my thoughts were rattling around in my head like pebbles in a tin can. Scratched and bruised I ran on.

Suddenly I went flying! I'd stepped into a mud-filled pothole with my short leg! There was no time to nurse bruised knees and a muddy face and hands. I scrambled out of there as fast as I could, spitting mud out of my mouth. Gross! There was mud in my nose, too. I cleared each nostril on the run. Double yuck!

I bit my teeth down hard because the pain was real. I wanted to lie down in the grass and scream! I staggered on as fast as I could. *"Please don't let him catch me,"* I cried over and over inside. I was gibbering and jabbering like a madman, tears, snot, and spit meeting on my chin... and dripping down. I was too tired to do anything about that. This was worse than doing a marathon without proper practice.

At last – the old mango tree – very leafy and a good place to hide. I carefully climbed up, so I'd leave no fresh leafy evidence at the bottom, just in case he was still after me. I gathered more scratches and bruises on the way up. Even my bruises had bruises.

But I was safe at last.

I used my shirt front to mop up my face. I smiled as I held my camera close to my chest. I thought of Uncle Benny who fell on his way home from the shebeen. He was carrying a bottle of wine but the wine stayed safe. He held it tightly so it didn't go flying. I had done the same with my camera when I fell.

Then I had the shock of my life… someone else was after me. The shout – it carried well, *"I'll catch him, boss. Thousand for me…yeah! Today…jackpot."* This was not a tired old man, but someone full of energy and hungry for the prize. So, there was a price on my head. I saw a poster in my mind: WANTED DEAD OR ALIVE: BOY WITH STOLEN CAMERA.

I felt like giggling again only this time tears poured out. I bit my lips, shut my eyes tight and sat there, stiff as a board.

"Hey, boy, where are you?"

"I'm finding you, boy."

More than one voice! I began to shake. What if they decided to look up into the trees? I was glad there were no mangoes on my tree. What if…? *No!* I scolded myself, *don't think like that!*

I wished I could control the shaking in my body. I was scared spitless. Then I had a real problem! My bladder refused to hold on any longer and I had a childish accident right there up in the mango tree. I closed my eyes and let it happen, tears flowing freely.

"Mom," I groaned. I had aches and pains all over. Now I had increased the problem. What if The Dudes found out I'd peed

179

myself? Shame. Disgrace. They'd rename me Hop-a-long-Pee-Jay, or something. Anyway PJ would get new meaning.

I should've gone to the movies. Why, Oh why didn't I go to the movies? I thought of Sapho. What would he do right now? Surely, he'd have a plan. I should've gone to watch Bucks play Birds with The Dudes. There's such a lot of things I could've done instead.

Then the runners were below me.

"Please, please, don't let them look up."

From where I was, I could see below. My green jacket blended in well with the leaves. None of them looked up – I counted four hopefuls. They ran on, shouting and laughing and having fun.

Then, for me, the pawpaw hit the fan! I pinched and squirmed and held on with all my might but nothing doing… I let rip. Fear like I never knew in my little life before had a strong hold on my insides.

They twisted and turned without pity.

If my chasers were close, they'd have heard… the sounds that came from my insides frightened even me. The smell was worse than I can describe. I wanted to vomit. I curled my camera strap around a strongish looking branch and decided enough was enough – I was going home. They were after a boy with a camera.

I wound my jacket tightly around the camera in case it rained. There were no monkeys around, but they may be around later and the curious little things may just decide to make off with my precious camera.

Slowly I climbed down, placing one foot carefully after the other, still shaking like a leaf in an August wind.

Then I saw it… a green mamba, slithering along the branch just below me. I froze. I nearly put my foot on it! My breathing almost stopped. I held on tightly. The snake lifted its head, and its forked tongue tested the air. If I breathed, I don't remember. Its upper half was swaying slowly in the air, its head almost alongside me. I shut my eyes tight. If I was going to be bitten by a snake, I didn't want to see it happen.

I tried to think of what we had been taught about local snakes. Green mambas were not as dangerous as black mambas, but their poison could kill a person. They feed on birds, birds' eggs, and other small mammals. They also feed on chameleons and lizards. Be nice if they finished them all!

For a long time, I remained motionless. Then I heard a scaly, slithering sound. I peeped and there was its tail disappearing among the leaves below me. With a thankful heart I began my downward climb. Speedily!

Suddenly an unholy noise broke out. The monkeys! They were on the way but seeing the snake gave them the shrieking heebie-jeebies. *Who or what likes snakes?* I wondered.

"*Snake! Snake!*" My chasers were returning! "*Da monkeys dey seen da snake!*" They set up a terrified yell and ran with all their might, until they saw me, almost at the base of the tree. They came to a sudden stop crashing comically into each other. Cursing and swearing they untangled themselves.

"Hey, you, boy, stop luffing! Where da boss's ca-mera what you stealing?"

"Cumaan, cumaan, where da ca-mera? Give it to me!"

"No-o-o, boy, you give me-e-e da ca-mera."

They squabbled among themselves and then turned on me again.

They all yelled at me then one of them stepped closer and stretched to grab me by the arms. His face showed pure horror. He spat. He shouted, "Ugh! Uya nuka! (you stink)." One by one his mates drew closer for a niff and shrank back in disgust. They then pinched their noses and came closer to inspect my backside. They drew back sickened by the sight.

I wanted to die.

181

"Where da boss's ca-mera?" screamed the one at the far end, still holding his nose.

"Wha-what camera?" I stuttered. "I haven't go-go-got no camera."

"You *lying*," shouted one of them, "we seen you. You took da boss's ca-mera."

I actually began to cry. Snivelling and snuffling I burst out, "I came to look for mangoes and a snake nearly bit me."

Things changed. They showed great sympathy and tried to come closer but quickly jumped back.

They spoke among each other and I made out they thought my state was brought on by fear. They agreed that they would have poo-ed in their pants, too, if they were almost bitten by a snake.

"Ag-a, shem, boy, sor-ree."

"Go home. You ver' lucky. Snake can keel you."

"Don' go for mangoes alone…ver' dangerous… *ingozi*."

They kept calling out until they were out of sight.

Then I ran as though the wind was carrying me along. I had to get to the shed. There was a tap behind it where I could clean up. I knew Mom would be in bed still. She stayed there until four o'clock sometimes because she also did her marking. Being the holiday, she was marking projects her learners had worked on during the term.

The neighbours must have all been in front of their TV's – Sharks were playing Blue Bulls that afternoon and no one missed the curtain-raisers. Football fans were in for a treat too – Bucks were up against Birds. Everyone knew who was going to win that match, but… you never know.

I was very pleased no one was outside.

I did the best I could to shower under the outside tap. The water seemed to be colder than ever. I shivered from the cold and the thoughts that ran around my head – what if… Then I used my filthy shirt as a sort of skirt and ran to have a proper shower inside.

"Peter-John… PJ, is that you?"

"Yes, Ma. I decided not to go to the movies. I'm going to the beach instead."

"Where are you from now?"

"I took a walk."

"Come here, let me see you."

I crossed my fingers and walked to Mom's room.

"Come," she patted the bed, "sit here by your Mama. She did the hardest Sudoku without making one mistake. Aren't you gonna congratulate her?"

"Oh, Mom, that's good. I know how much you like doing the hard ones."

"Yep, you call me an addict. I suppose I am one. Some of those games in the hard section take more than an hour to finish."

I tried my best to concentrate on Mom's voice, but the rats were back in full force. Killer ruled my thoughts. Was he still around? Would he recognise me? Would I recognise him? Would any of those men remember me? My frizzy white mop that stuck out in all directions would not be easily forgotten. I had a feeling he would send them back to look for me. What if those money-hungry dudes came into the township and went from door to door? Worse still what if he took them from door to door with him? Where did they come from? Must be part of the busloads of weekenders or day-trippers who filled the place. They were complete strangers to me.

That camera held Killer's evil secret. He wanted it so badly he would kill us for it. There were no other boys in the woods. Those men found only me. What if they took the man to the tree and he got them to climb it? *No-o-o-o!*

Killer would just have to stop anyone in the township. "I'm looking for a boy with white hair."

My white hair would be the giveaway. There is a difference between blonde and white and my hair is white!

The 'what if's" chased each other round and round my head. In case they did search the township, I'd go out. Mom never answered the door on Saturdays especially. Friends and family called first.

"You don't look yourself, PJ; what's the matter, boy? Are those scratches on your cheeks? Your arms!"

"I'm okay, Ma. It's just that everyone is watching sport and I don't like it. Oh, and I was on the short cut and raced into a tree that had a hanging branch." I hated lying to my mother.

"Talk about watching sport...the news...," she looked at her watch, "put on the transistor on the tallboy behind you, and let's hear East Coast's local news."

We were just in time to hear about the beach murders. Anyone who had any helpful information was asked to contact the police as soon as possible. I must have shown something because Mom said,

"No need to worry, Son. The cops'll get the dirty dogs. Those poor men. I hope they don't have small children."

I had to get out of the house! If Killer did a house search it was the end of me... of us.

"Okay, then, Mums, I'm off again. I want to go to the internet café." I grabbed my black FBI cap from the hall stand and slapped it on back to front to hide my crop of white frizzy hair. Rashid, in my class, says FBI stands for full blooded Indian. *Very* funny...

Then I had a better idea. I had a knitted Rasta cap with dreadlocks tied to the rim that would cover my head quite completely. My mop gave it fullness and the dreadlocks completed the picture. I smiled and felt a bit safer. My first time wearing it. I just didn't like the look of it and wearing it may make me look like a dagga smoker. I'm no man's judge but there are some things I find hard to handle. Ma would have a fit if she saw me, but that was not as bad as what I feared would happen.

184

"Enjoy yourself. One of these days we'll have our very own computer – just you wait and see." Her voice sounded like she was trying to concentrate on what she was doing.

"See you later."

"Make sure you're home before sunset."

"I know the drill, Ma," I called out.

Off I sped, taking the long route. I shouted a greeting to the few 'aunts' and 'uncles' and 'oumas' and 'oupas' seated on their verandahs as I passed, as well as the noisy girls and boys who were playing football in the dusty street. They knew me too well to be put off by my disguise. A few tried to stop me, shouting, *Rastaman* and *Bob Marley* and *Burning Spear*. One old man seated on his verandah shouted, "Rastaman, you gotta spliff for a ole man?" and he cracked out laughing. I just waved and hurried on. I beathed a thankful prayer that they were not there to see me when I sneaked home.

Two or more cars raced by, raising clouds of dust, in a hurry to be seated in front of their tv screens for the curtain raisers. The street players scattered, shouting crazily about who should get the ball when the game carried on. Taxis hurrying into the 'Ship, hooted long and loud, warning the street players off.

At last… the beachfront take-away café. I got myself a burger and chips and a drink. I boldly sprinted to the pier. I sat staring into the blueness in front of me seeing a mango tree instead. The monkeys had hold of the camera and they had managed to open the flap and one of them was chewing on the SIM card. The zoom nozzle was hanging down uselessly. My whole body shook. The rats in the ceiling were having a wild wrestling match.

Just why I had returned to the pier I couldn't understand. What did I hope to see? Why was it so necessary to come back here to the spot where I had witnessed a real-life shooting? Shootings happened all the time, in the movies and in the township. Now I actually saw a man raise a gun and shoot three human beings that he knew. I felt

185

sick. Was I going to be his next victim? Just where *was* this going to end?

Shouldn't I go find my camera and know for sure if it was still there? I should take it to the police especially after hearing that newscast. On TV I saw many times how specialists got information from footage that was destroyed. Maybe that was just TV? But technology made a lot of things possible.

Where was the killer man right now? Did he find his goods untouched when he got back to his boat? Had he left by the time the police came on the scene?

My mind had never been this noisy.

There was a small sign of the morning's happenings. Crime scene tape fixed to a rock was snaking and snapping in the wind like a giant ribbon. I tore open my food packet and took up a burning hot chip.

I blew gently on it. I had just put it into my mouth when a large, swaying movement caught the corner of my eye.

Killer! My stomach knotted painfully. He was making straight for my bench. I wanted to hurl. I breathed deeply and chewed slowly before swallowing painfully. I thought I'd choke. I needed a drink. Quickly I took a swallow of my peach-flavoured water. *Gotta control my stomach.* My food suddenly smelled grossly unpleasant.

He plonked himself down next to me, breathing heavily like a long-distance runner. The fat folds seemed to go on flip-flopping even after he was seated. I looked at his face. He was as red as a tomato and his chins hung over his collar. He put his hands on his thighs, leaned forward and soon his breathing slowed down. He looked at me.

"Hello, my boy." He spoke very kindly. He was being friendly. I wasn't fooled. There were people around.

I cleared my choked-up throat. "Hello, Sir," I whispered. My heart was hammering, and my ears were ringing. What to do? The police needed to be in on this. What I knew had to be told to the right people!

"Didn't we meet earlier on, son?"

Son? I was not *his* son! "We did? Where?"

"Oh, I don't know…maybe in the Post Office…the bank…down on the beach by the pier?"

I turned to look him full in the face. "You're a fisherman?" and my eyes fell to his huge belly… on purpose.

He threw back his head and laughed merrily. His whole body bounced up and down as though he was made of rubber.

Then softly he said, "No, child, I was not on the pier, I was in my boat down on the beach with some… um… er … friends. I saw a boy up here on the bench. On this very bench? He looked rather like you…"

He turned, snatched off my cap and said, "Yep! Same white bush." Now his whisper was a frightening snarl.

I was like jelly in a bowl.

"You're making a mistake, Sir," I was afraid to shout or to talk loudly. I felt he would hurt me if I drew attention to us. He could easily say I had stolen his camera and he wanted it back.

This time he would have enough listeners. I even recognised a few families there…Tommy Brown and his mother and brothers were there – fishing from the pier. I remembered – they fished every Saturday and on Sunday afternoon after church. His mother still sent Mom a fish now and then when they had a good catch. Mrs Brown never heard about my fight with Tommy. I think he was ashamed to tell her that a smaller boy had given him those wounds. One of his brothers told his classmate that Tommy was mugged in a lonely street in town.

I felt really sick inside.

Suddenly help was right there... a policeman in uniform walked past us, holding his little son, Craig, by the hand... what's more I knew him! He was a deacon in our church!

"*Hey... Craig*," I shouted, too loudly.

Father and son turned. I jumped from my seat, burst into tears and blurted out: "*Arrest him, arrest that man...he's this morning's killer.*" I pointed at the man. He turned turkey red. He opened his mouth to speak but his words fell out making no sense. Then he managed to shout, "Let the little tyke prove it!"

"Yes," I said, "let's prove it. I have it all on camera."

"Liar! He stole that camera from me. Where's it, hey, where's my camera?"

"You know I didn't steal it." I turned to Brother Dickens. "Don't let him get away. I saw him shoot three men and he even took a shot at me when he saw me." From the corner of my eye I saw Tommy and his brothers in the crowd that had gathered around us. The Township Daily (TTD for short), or gossip vine, would fly faster than ever. East Coast news would be thrilling, with PJ catcher of a killer. I hoped Mom would understand.

"Where be the camera, Little Brother?"

I told Brother Dickens everything except the embarrassing parts.

"Come, cuff him then I'll show you."

Killer flopped down like a punctured balloon.

Whew!

A crowd had gathered, and Brother Dickens had enough back-up if the man tried to escape. He made a phone call, and a black Maria was there in no time flat. Killer was handcuffed and put into the back of the van. He didn't go quietly. Big and strong as he was, he wasn't able to shake himself loose from the hold on him. What came out of his mouth was enough to make a sailor ashamed. I didn't dare look at him.

I led Brother Dickens and two other policemen to the mango tree. I laughed out loud to see that the monkeys had not done any of the damage my mind had made up. I hope I didn't turn red when the policeman who climbed up the tree said, "Pooh! Something smells bad around here."

Part 3
Schools opened that Monday. Sapho gave me a huge conspiratorial wink when we met. He waved his pinkie and index finger at me and then pointed at his brand-new watch. With a loud laugh, he ducked into the boys' toilet. When I saw him in class a little later on, he had a black eye and guess what - no watch! *Whiskers!* I thought. *Where's the watch?*

Soon I noticed Sapho was engrossed in something he was writing behind a curled hand. Uh-oh, I thought, he's hiding something. It could only be gang news. Surely it had something to do with the black eye and the missing watch? Will I be included when the note is passed around? I wondered. I thought not, as I was never included when violence was in the air, and I was sure he was on a vengeance trail and was taking The Dudes along. Imagine my surprise when, wonder of wonders, it came to me, too.

Meet me behind the boys' toilet first break. Serious happenings.

He didn't have to sign it: we all knew his terrible scrawl and his frightening spelling! I just knew it had to do with the obvious forceful disappearance of the watch. I was fairly sure I knew the identity of the "thief". What a thing - the thief had been knocked off! Irony of ironies, I guess one could say. I tried hard to concentrate on the lessons and was reprimanded twice by Ms Frazer for not paying attention. She'd asked me a question and I'd not even heard her call my name! Fear, excitement, apprehension all filled my quivering

189

insides. Would I have to fight, too, to get the watch back? I just could not think of it as Saps's watch.

My mind flashed back to Pastor's sermon yesterday. He addressed young people especially and spoke at length about peer pressure. He mentioned having to change your friends if need be in order to keep the devil off your back. Change my friends? I couldn't think of that right now. Admittedly my friends skewed sharply toward the delinquent side, but they didn't put any undue pressure on me - *I* put pressure on *me*. They were my friends and I liked them. A lot. Unconditionally.

Sometimes I became very confused especially about the unconditional love thing. Was it showing unconditional love, leaving them because they were wayward? And wayward they were; some of the boys had problems in their homes like you wouldn't believe. Talk about abuse! Some of them were whipped at least once a week. They never reported it, because, as one of them said, "Bad parents are better than no parents." I daren't comment. Having no father is bad enough. They stole to eat, to dress, to pay school fees and to support drug habits. Yes, most of The Dudes were dagga addicts. If Mom found out.... Perish the thought. If ever there were victims of circumstance, The Dudes, at least most of them, were. I counted myself blessed - VERY blessed.

"Peter-John, would you mind returning to the present? You are very far from us today."

"Sorry, Miss. I'm really sorry."

"Gone fishing, I suppose?"

"Something like that, Miss," I replied.

"Well, consider that to be the one that got away and come back to us. You'll go catch it after school."

The class had a good laugh at me. I reddened, nodded, and tried to concentrate.

She was Mom's friend, and I didn't want her asking questions, or telling Mom about me and my preoccupation in the classroom. I made a great, big effort and was soon engrossed in her lesson. It was about Macbeth, my favourite Shakespearean, so it wasn't all that hard.

When the siren went, I had mixed feelings - so mixed, I had to make a beeline for the lavatory and gave a heartfelt prayer of thanks for the clump of tissues Mom always insisted I keep in my pocket. I heartily wished I had a can of spray especially when someone called out: someone's had a dead thing inside them for ages and decided to poop it out today! *Sies!*

Embarras*sing.*

Sheepishly I went to wash my hands, not looking anyone in the eye. Then I became resentful: why should I be apologetic about a human function? With head held high, I walked out to look for the gang.

"Oh, there you are..."

"When you gotta go, you gotta go," I chipped in. "What gives? What've I missed?"

I put on a show of bravado, trying hard not to let my nervousness show through. I hated any kind of showdown - just not my scene. My gut told me there was BIG TROUBLE ahead.

Saps looked at me. "This morning, in the toilet, Tommy Brown took my watch from me. *(I knew it!)* He had his sidekicks with him, and they did me over. Look at my eye. What'm I gonna tell my mudder?" His body language was extremely funny. "She gonna freak if she year anything. I tole de udders bout Saturday, PJ..." Udders! Very funny. "De BIG THING now, is to teach Tommy and co a lesson. They think that just because Tommy is so huge and tall, everyone's scared of him. Well, I'm not!"

"What we gonna do?" asked Skins Pearson. His real name was Robin but he was called Skins because he was so skinny. He was the newest addition to the gang. Newly from Durban and full of stories!

"D-d-d-do? D-do?" thundered Thabo. "We're g-g-g-gonna r-rip their hearts out and th-th-throw them to the dogs!" He was so mad that the spit flew as he spluttered and stuttered.

"You've sprayed it," laughed Temba. "FIGHTING time," he whooped. "Let's name the time and day."

"And weapons, don't forget," from Lexie.

"Yeah, weapons," said Sakkie. "We going to *klaar* (finish) them. *Vandag gaan hulle sien met wie foeter hulle.* Today they gonna see with who they interfering." He often repeated himself in English when he spoke Afrikaans as if we did not understand it. "Whatchu say, *ou* PJ? You game? We need the whole gang for this. No sleeping partners this time, *ek sê.*"

"*Ja, jong,* it's time to test your muscles," said Ray, another newbie who resented my being a 'passive' member. He spoke with a mock sneer and made a dive to feel my biceps. I shrugged him off.

"Remember Tommy…" someone started to say.

"… Yay, PJ got it in him." Someone else chipped in.

"But he fights his own fights," I said sternly. "When we had that fight, things were very different. But he's got a nerve! He knows Saps is my friend. Maybe he's sending a message to me."

Ray got to hear about *the fight.*

"Don't make this your personal fight, PJ. Sapho is a gang member so it's all of us he's after." Ray had a mean look in his dark brown eyes when he said that to me. For a boy, he has extra-long, thick eyelashes. "We taking on the whole gang, and there's a special something for the dirt-bag whose fist connected Saps's eye," he announced waving his fist in the air.

"I don't even know who it was… " began Saps.

"...then they'll all get a special something." I swear Ray has Rottweiler blood! He can be quite vicious. However, he is always patient and kind to the gang members and he treats females like they are made of glass. Once I heard him tell someone who commented on his treatment of girls, "Cool it! My mother's a girl, isn't she? And my sister's a girl, huh?" I've respected Ray for that ever since, though I must admit I am more than a little afraid of him. Afraid, but safe around him.

They were all looking at me. I daren't show any reluctance; feelings were high, and a tidal wave of anger radiated from their very pores!

It made my skin crawl.

My tummy began to twist. I had to think fast. This was one time I did NOT want to experience any 'gang excitement'. I had to keep from getting into the news at all costs.

There had to be another way. I had to think on the run.

"Why don't we try another way?" I asked, looking around at everyone. "If we get him into trouble with the law, he'll be hurt even more, don't you think?" I looked around hoping the desperation in my heart didn't reveal itself in my voice. I had to think. It was hard, thinking and talking all at the same time.

"Shoot. Let's hear it."

"What?"

"Go on, say what's on your mind, *my lightie*!" (my little boy – affectionately derogatory)

I let them discuss possible alternatives to violence but could think of almost nothing acceptable to a blood-thirsty crew. They bombarded me with questions for a little while, and I tried to answer, waffling and humming and hawing, playing for time, and then the idea dropped! Would they buy it? They were baying for blood right now and my way involved no violence. I took a deep breath and looked around at everyone.

"Well, we know how Saps got the watch in the first place don't we?"

"What's your point?" growled Saps.

"Yeah, whatchu getting at?" snapped Ray.

"Looks like *boytjie* here got no plan at all" drawled Luke, who spoke very little but had a bad temper and quick, painful fists. He was reputed to be fast and skilful with a knife as well. Luke was a member who had joined at the very beginning but had left for The East Cape. He was back now because the job his father left to do had finished.

"Cool it, guys. Listen to me..."

"...we're listening, and we ain't hearing nothing," laughed Harry. He was called Harriet by everyone, except the gang members, behind his back because he had girlish mannerisms.

Harry could fight, though, and he was not afraid of anything or anyone. He bragged that if he could get into the ring with Mr Brookes, the principal, he'd have him in the first round. I don't think any of the boys believed him. Mr Brookes walked on the balls of his feet like a boxer. Even the easy way he swung his arms when he walked made me suspect he was a practicing sportsman. His physique alone would deter most men, but, apparently, not Harry. He called himself Dirty Harry because he was a dirty fighter, he said. Truth to tell, no one in the group could remember seeing Harry fight. Personally, I suspected that he made a lot of noise to frighten off prospective opponents. Something like a noisy poodle - you know, those little house dogs that create a real din. Maybe someday I'd be proved wrong about him?

"That new security guard is just longing to catch someone shoplifting. What if we tell her anonymously, of course, that Tommy stole from her shop? She wants to teach someone a lesson real bad - make an example of them - and I'm sure they'll call in the police."

"Hmm, tell us more. Sounds like an idea," said one of the boys.

"NAY *EK SE*! I want to eat him up with these two!" yelled Ray, holding up his clenched fists.

"Cool it, Ray-Ray," said Luke, soothingly. "It would be real nice if he spent a night or two in the chookie." He began to laugh and soon everyone was rolling around, slapping each other's shoulders and high fiving each other wildly.

When the laughter died down Sapho looked at me. "Siren's about to go. We'll meet this afternoon when we get together to do our homework. Then we'll work out the details." He held up his hand for a high five and, mercifully, the siren sent us rushing off.

I had some careful, convincing strategising to do. My future with the gang was on the line, and homework or no homework, they seemed determined, this time to include me in the gang's activities. Deep inside I felt very resentful - Sapho had stolen the dratted thing in the first place - why not just let it go? Of course, there was the question of the black eye: that had to be avenged! I agreed about that. From a muffled distance I heard Pastor's preaching voice, *"Vengeance is mine, saith the LORD."*

What is it they say about casting pearls before swine? I fervently wished I lived in Siberia.

It was pay-back time, and I had the unenviable task of thinking up an alternative to violence that would appease the bloodlust of my mates. After school I made an excuse about an errand into town and cut short the homework session. Thabo was good at Math and I left them to his not-so-tender mercies. Fortunately, no one thought to ask what I was going to do in town.

I needed to think, and the plan had to work. This calls for some creativity and a huge truck load of luck, I thought. Where in the name of all that's wonderful do script writers get their ideas?

I made a bee line for the pier. The Dudes would hardly leave what they were doing to check that I was indeed going to the taxi rank, would they? I took the chance, anyway. If push came to shove, I'd simply tell them that I had some thinking to do and needed to be on my own. Why would they fight with that - we were friends, weren't we ... we were entitled to time out weren't we? I just needed time out, that's all.

I ran along the path that led to the fishing pier. Puffing and panting, I flopped into the spot I found. I gazed out to sea, enjoying the antics of the gulls and the activity on the pier. Yet all the while my mind was busy. I had to make sure that I got home before Mom did. Her school was on the other end of town and she never got home before five. She liked to do all her marking at school, and, being Head of the English Department, made sure all the day's paperwork was done before leaving. If there was a staff meeting, she got home even later.

My mind was busy: concocting strategies, checking them over and rejecting them one after the other. One was too obvious, another too risky and so on. What on earth was I going to do? I tried to remind myself just why these guys were my friends. Wasn't this a good time to end all relations? I wished with all my heart that I'd never met them.

I jumped up and ran along the pier, careful not to disturb the anglers' tackle and stuff. When an unexpected, huge wave thundered up, saturating everyone on the pier, I gasped but was exhilarated! I ran on and came out at the other end, wet but feeling better. My head was clearer. I sat on the steps again.

Thoughts of the killing I had witness in this very place made me shiver. That was a bad experience, but things worked out well in that the Killer was sent to prison for a long, long time. The money he had stolen and the drugs he had kept back were issues that were still

196

written about in the newspapers and on the news casts. The families of the dead men felt that they should be considered when that money was being decided upon. Between the three widows there were eight children ranging in age from a few months to thirteen.

Suddenly the germ of an idea that was birthed at school began to germinate, like a little light was turned on and was getting brighter and brighter. It began slowly to grow just as if I had no control over my own mind! It seemed so simple, so logical. I began to feel bad about regretting my friendship with The Dudes. They were quite nice guys under the hard, self-protective veneer, knocked there by circumstances. Victims of circumstances beyond their control - that's what they were. How does one stop being a victim and become a victor? In their case, exactly how would they go about it? Truth to tell, I found them interesting. They added colour to my almost sterile world.

Don't get me wrong… I cannot bear the thought of becoming anything that'd bring heartache to my mother and disgrace to the family name. My present situation was bad enough. Just how was I going to get this plan into gear? Tommy had no business interfering with Sapho unless he was indirectly trying to cause it with me.

Perhaps he had a secret plan for me…

I began to concentrate on the germ of a plan that was niggling at the back of my mind. If we planned carefully and each of us played his part according to plan, it should go perfectly. Tommy would be carted off to jail and that would be that. No assault charges…. Nothing.

I sprinted back home just as the boys were deciding to give up on me. Panting like a dog in the shade, I told them the plan. It was decided that Friday would be the best day as it meant that guy would spend the whole weekend in the chookie.

"I got a uncle dere by de cop shop," said Sakkie. Great. He'd make sure the boy spent the weekend there.

197

Ray was not at all convinced. "Wanna see my knuckles bleeding, from bashing his teeth in," he grumbled. The Dudes laughed and dismissed his words. I was greatly relieved that they went with my plan.

At school the following day, Tommy walked about with a swagger.

He must have thought he'd won the war. He had another thought coming.

The following day was Friday and… Action! Tommy had no idea the watch had been stolen so he was in for it. I went up to the security lady that afternoon and told her that a boy would come in the following day wearing a watch she may recognise.

"He's a crook," I told her, "and he often carries a knife, so be careful." She glared at me with unfriendly eyes staring almost through me. She remembered our first meeting.

"His name is Tommy," I said keeping my voice and expression as unfriendly as hers.

That brought her up quickly. "I know him… that tall boy with a lotta brothers?"

"Yip." I nodded and walked away. Then I turned back abruptly. "Don't get him today. He only carries a knife on Fridays. The police must find the knife in his pocket." I kept a very straight face.

She grinned and nodded her head rapidly. My new best-friend-to-be?

The following afternoon we followed Tommy and his crew closely as we walked home. As we neared the shop, Sapho called out, "How's it, ou Toms, can I buy you a cool drink just to show no hard feelings."

"Or maybe a beer," Ray sneered meanly.

"I don't drink beer," Tommy said, standing still. Then he turned around. "No hard feelings, hey? Why should I believe you when you with your sidekicks? Whatchu planning?"

"Not planning nothing, ou," Sapho said. I thought *how right you are*. Double negative and all that. "We just want peace coz we all live together," Sapho said very convincingly, I thought. The Dudes muttered words no one would have made out, but it sounded like they agreed. I mimed nothing that made sense.

Tommy turned to his brothers. "Go home, lighties… now!"

They raced off.

We walked into the shop and the security guard waited a few minutes until we had all chosen drinks from the fridges and then she waited until we were outside the cash register area.

She walked up to Tommy and asked him if she could have a closer look at the watch that he was wearing. He looked at her in surprise and stretched out his arm. We stood back from them and looked on very seriously.

She called the manager, and he came over on the trot. Seeing schoolboys had his aerial on high alert.

"Look this watch, Sir," she said nervously.

"Yow! Same as the one missing from the display case over there."

Tommy became very uneasy. He started to stutter and mutter denial. "I… I… I…"

The manager held him by the wrist that had the watch and pulled him forcefully to the office at the back. The security guard helped to control the struggling boy. Only when they were behind the closed door did we rejoice. High fives and back slaps and hair pulling amidst muted shouts of victory. Then we raced outside to really shout for joy.

Suddenly we heard the sirens. They had really called the police! The Black Maria pulled up with a screech and four policemen tumbled out.

"Four policemen for one schoolboy," I breathed, shocked.

"Yisslaik," Sakkie exploded.

Soon they came out with the handcuffed howling, protesting boy. When he caught sight of Sapho, he shouted, "Tell them, Saps... tell them. Please.... Tell them."

"I got nothing to tell them, ou Toms... nu'*ting*.'

We watched him being shoved into the back of the Black Maria along with two of the policemen.

Of course, TTD made sure the news spread... like wildfire. Comments flew around like feathers from a pillow ripped apart in the wind. Opinions varied and some were downright cruel.

One old man said, "They must throw away the key!" Tommy and his brothers had tied a cracker to the old man's dog's tail one Guy Fawkes Day. That was a pitiful sight to see. The details don't bear repeating. Tommy denied it but the old man knew what he saw. Oupa Dyke never replaced his dog. He openly said, when people offered to get him another, "For that lout to kill him, too? No, thank you. I will live without a dog."

My life changed. Mother has a way of interrogating that'll bring the truth out of a solid rock! Out came the story of my friendship with The Dudes. She listened to my answers and as the questions became deeper and deeper – I fed her question 'bag' for my answers gave rise to more questions – the whole story came out. Mum said nothing at all to judge me or the boys. She simply nodded her head and continued with the questions, until finally...

"Well, my boy, that's an earful. We'll talk again. I need to digest all of this."

A week later, at the dinner table, mom reached across and said, with shiny eyes as though she wanted to cry, "I'm ginne miss you so much, my baby."

I stared at her open-mouthed. I had to close up, chew and swallow. Swallowing partly chewed food made me choke. She slapped my back and gave me water.

"Whatchu mean, Mum? Where're you going?"

"Where'm I going? No, my baby… where are *you* going? Saint Jude's Boarding School for Boys, in the Cape, has accepted you. A finer boarding school for boys does not exist. Since it's still so early in this second term they have accepted you. Your teachers have all sung loudly and well about your performance and the Principal Brookes is closely related to that principal. All arrangements have been made." She stared into my eyes without blinking. I started back like a rat completely hypnotised by a predator. My mouth was dry, and my appetite completely gone. No wonder she had prepared my favourite things to eat. This was a farewell meal.

"The wonders of technology… I have even your new uniform and everything else they mention in their list for beginners. So, it's off to boarding school early in the morning. We fly there and I'll fly back tomorrow night."

End of story. No time for tears. Shall keep a diary when I'm there. I have memories that will stick then, hopefully, I'll not be making killer decisions when I grow up. I am grateful for having a single mother who has put the brakes om me from small.

Man – the misfit species
Rogers Atukunda

"Man, The Misfit Species...Man the so-called rational and social animal is actually man the neurotic (foolish) animal, because his rationality is completely misapplied, and his societies are distressed and crumbling"-Sampradaya Dasa, "Intellectual Animalism": 1983, p5.

Evolutionists, archaeologists, and anthropologists trace the origin of humans from the Miocene epoch, a time when fossils (the physical evidence of a prehistoric organism, often comprising a shell, bone, or another durable skeletal part, which in the majority of cases belongs to an extinct species; Richard Fortey, 2005) were transformed into ape-like creatures out of which human beings evolved.

Human evolution: the biological and cultural development of humans and related species, is mainly evidenced by a large number of fossil bones and teeth that have been found at various places throughout Africa, Europe, and Asia (Chris Stringer, 2005).

These theorists seem to suggest that all humans have similar origins despite the separation of present-day continents. The differences in body shape, colour, language and behaviour can be attributed to the varying climates.

Multilingualism can also be closely traced from the Tower of Babel (Christian perspective) where it is believed that God hurled at the architects various strange languages to confuse and prevent them from building a tower that threatened to reach his palace, up there in heaven and "possibly spy on him". That is how humans were scattered all over the face of earth.

Considering the biblical version of human evolution, a super being called God created one man Adam and later crafted a woman, Eve, out of Adam's rib. The two pro-created and filled the world.

Likewise, according to Greek myths and legends; plants, animals and gods are all inventions of the supreme god, Zeus. It was Prometheus, one of the Titans and son to the Titan Iapetus by the sea nymph Clymene who created humans. All these versions of creation share a similar ideal; that is, the fact that all creations sprung from one source and that all humans sprung from one being.

From this obscure exposition, the implication is clear. That we are the same: a similar structure; two legs, arms, eyes, ears, nostrils, lips and one head. The ethnicities in which we belong (ed) mean (t) that we are/were of the same race, custom, language and religion living in a particular area.

The actual question is: what are we? And how did we get involved in aggressive rivalries?

What Is Man?

"What a piece of art is man!" wondered Prince Hamlet in Shakespeare's play, Hamlet (1601). Philosophers, writers and other wise men have for centuries tried to demystify the complexity of this creature called man, but to no avail. God himself must be scratching his grey haired-head and caressing his long white beard while reflecting and wondering about what exactly he created in this thing, man!

From his essay, "What Is Man?", Mark Twain (Samuel Langhorne Clemens) puzzles with the question of man through a dialogue between an Old Man and a Young Man.

"The Old Man had asserted that the human being is merely a machine, and nothing more. The Young Man objected, and asked him to go into particulars and furnish his reasons for his position."
Then the old man of course suggested the various instances in which man behaves more like a machine rather than a human. Agreeably, man can be cold, cruel and capricious as I shall soon expose in detail. George Orwell, in his novel "Animal Farm" (1945), through Old Major's speech, suggests that man is simply a parasite, an accident in nature. You can understand man only by equating or likening him to jiggers, fleas, lice, bedbugs, leeches, ticks and other sorts of pests.
Major (the prize boar) clearly explains man's parasitical nature stressing the fact that man only consumes yet he produces nothing. Man cannot lay eggs or produce milk or meat. He does not contribute anything to nature. Should we, therefore, conclude that man is a tick, flea or bedbug, etc.?

According to Albert Einstein (1954), a human being is part of the whole called by us universe, a part limited in time and space.

He writes: "We experience ourselves, our thoughts and feelings as something separate from the rest. A kind of optical delusion of consciousness. This delusion is a kind of prison for us, restricting us to our personal desires and to affection for a few persons nearest to us. Our task must be to free ourselves from the prison by widening our circle of compassion to embrace all living creatures and the whole of nature in its beauty. The true value of a human being is determined by the measure and the sense in which they have obtained liberation from the self. We shall require a substantially new manner of thinking if humanity is to survive."

To Einstein, this creature called man thinks it is intellectually above other creations but thinks only and only about self or self-desires! Sampradaya Dasa in his book, "Intellectual Animalism" (1983) clearly suggests that man is an animal. He supports this suggestion by explaining man's impulsive nature-driven towards fulfilment of the survival instincts, generally considered to be animal instincts.

"Everywhere in the world, human beings have four basic requirements. We all must have food to eat, a place to sleep, opportunity for sexual intercourse, and an adequate means of defence." (Dasa: 1).

He clarifies that the basic principles which govern animal existence are eating, sleeping, mating and defending, and concludes that the human social body can't claim greater achievement than that automatically achieved by lower species.

"The bird will make his home high in the tree; man will make his home high in a skyscraper. Man will wage war from inside tanks; the rhinoceros will use its own armour. Although the technology and degree of sophistication are different, the basic activities are the same." (Dasa: 3).

Dasa argues that all our efforts, brainwork, science and invention are driven towards achieving the four animal needs. Man is thought to have an advantage over other animals i.e., his ability to reason and yet this reasoning is useless.

Dasa develops his argument thus: unfortunately, our human milestones are frustration, dissatisfaction, and anxiety, which culminate in arguments, violence, disturbed social systems, and ultimately international war.

Herbert Marcuse, in his text, "One Dimensional Man" (1964), suggests that modern man is a robot, a product of automation. This concurs with Mark Twain's assertion that man is a machine because modern man is devoid of all feeling and humanness.

Modern man is manufactured and scientifically generated. He can appear in a fluid or metallic form or a computer-generated organism. He is a futuristic creature; a cyborg, a predator, a terminator, a clone, an avatar or a green alien, controlled by a one-dimensional technological thought. His existence has been 'pacified' and conditioned to respond to survival needs.

"Man today can do more than the culture heroes and half-gods..." (Marcuse p59), but he has, in the process, "lost his humanism, autonomous personality and the possibility of romantic love".

Under what Marcuse terms as "The Happy Consciousness", what new forms of control like radios, televisions and newspapers present and determine as freedom, truth, happiness, fulfilment and humanism is what modern man accepts as reality.

Marcuse argues that, "if man has learned to see and know what really is, he will act in accordance with truth" (p106).

Is this plausible in our new world where automated modern man has been manipulated into believing that 'the negative is positive, the inhuman is human and that enslavement is liberation'?

Therefore, man, the social animal, is actually a misfit species. Man is truly a neurotic or stupid organism!

Adapted from "Multi-Continental Affair" by Rogers Atukunda, BA Literature/English Makerere University, Kampala-Uganda.

Mmap Multi-disciplinary Series

If you have enjoyed *MEN: An International Anthology of African and Latin American Writers Vol 3*, consider these other fine books in the **Mmap Multi-disciplinary Series** from *Mwanaka Media and Publishing:*

Africanization and Americanization Anthology Volume 1, Searching for Interracial, Interstitial, Intersectional and Interstates Meeting Spaces, Africa Vs North America by Tendai R Mwanaka
A Conversation..., A Contact by Tendai Rinos Mwanaka
Africa, UK and Ireland: Writing Politics and Knowledge Production Vol 1 by Tendai R Mwanaka
Writing Language, Culture and Development, Africa Vs Asia Vol 1 by Tendai R Mwanaka, Wanjohi wa Makokha and Upal Deb
Zimbolicious: An Anthology of Zimbabwean Literature and Arts, Vol 3 by Tendai Mwanaka
Drawing Without Licence by Tendai R Mwanaka
Writing Grandmothers/ Escribiendo sobre nuestras raíces: Africa Vs Latin America Vol 2 by Tendai R Mwanaka and Felix Rodriguez
Tiny Human Protection Agency by Megan Landman
Ghetto Symphony by Mandla Mavolwane
A Portrait of Defiance by Tendai Rinos Mwanaka
Nationalism: (Mis)Understanding   Donald Trump's Capitalism, Racism, Global Politics, International Trade and Media Wars, Africa V's North America Vol 2 by Tendai R Mwanaka
Ouafa and Thawra: About a Lover From Tunisia by Arturo Desimone
Zimbolicious: An Anthology of Zimbabwean Literature and Arts, Vol 4 by Tendai Mwanaka and Jabulani Mzinyathi
Chitungwiza Mushamukuru Anthology by Tendai Rinos Mwanaka
The Day and the Dweller: A Study of the Emerald Tablets by Jonathan Thompson

Zimbolicious: An Anthology of Zimbabwean Literature and Arts, Vol 5 by Tendai Mwanaka

Robotics Anthology, Africa vs Asia Vol 2 by Tendai Rinos Mwanaka

Shaping Up by Tendai Rinos Mwanaka

Zimbolicious Anthology Vol 6: An Anthology of Zimbabwean Literature and Arts by Tendai Rinos Mwanaka and Chenjerai Mhondera

Registers of Loss: PhotoTalking to the Baobab Trees of Nyatate by Tendai Rinos Mwanaka

The Trick is to Keep Breathing: Covid 19 Stories From African and North American Writers, vol 3 by Tendai Rinos Mwanaka

Fixing Earth: An Anthology of Ireland, UK and Africa Writers, Vol 2 by Tendai Rinos Mwanaka

Zimbolicious: An Anthology of Zimbabwean Literature and Arts, Vol 7 Tendai Rinos Mwanaka and Tanaka Chidora

Writing Woman Anthology: Personal Essays and Short stories, An Anthology of African and Asian Writers, Vol 3 by Tendai Rinos Mwanaka, Abigail George, Sue Zhu and Monalisa Jena

Writing Woman Anthology: Drama and Scholarly Essays, An Anthology of African and Asian Writers, Vol 3 by Tendai Rinos Mwanaka, Abigail George, Sue Zhu and Monalisa Jena

WRITING WOMAN ANTHOLOGY: Poetry and Visual art by Tendai Rinos Mwanaka, Abigail George, Sue Zhu and Monalisa Jena

Zimbolicious: An Anthology of Zimbabwean Literature and Arts, Vol 8 by Tendai Rinos Mwanaka and Matthew Kunashe Chikono

Of poets, gods, ghosts. Irritants and storytellers by Tendai Rinos Mwanaka

The Aporia of Unnamed Things by Tendai Rinos Mwanaka

Men: An Anthology of African and Latin American writers vol 3 by Tendai Rinos Mwanaka and Ingrid Bringas

Glyphs of Love by Tendai Rinos Mwanaka

https://facebook.com/MwanakaMediaAndPublishing/